NEVIN HALICI'S

TURKISH

COOKBOOK

NEVIN HALICI'S
TURKISH
COOKBOOK

DORLING KINDERSLEY · LONDON

DEDICATION

Ağabeyim Feyzi Halıcı'ya

A Jill Norman Book

First published in Great Britain in 1989
by Dorling Kindersley Limited
9 Henrietta Street, London WC2E 8PS

British Library Cataloguing in Publication Data
Halici, Nevin
   Nevin Halici's Turkish cooking
   1. Food: Turkish dishes. Recipes
   I. Title
   641.59561

ISBN 0–86318–390–5

Translation by E.M. Samy
Designed by Bridgewater Design Ltd
Artwork by Lorraine Harrison
Photographs by Timuçin Tulgar
Additional photographs by Roland Michaud, pages:
11, 22, 35, 38, 51, 58, 90, 95, 110, 143, 154 © John Hillelson Agency

Colour reproduction by Colourscan, Singapore
Printed in Italy by A. Mondadori Editore, Verona

◊ CONTENTS ◊

◊ FOREWORD ◊

CLAUDIA RODEN

Nevin Halıcı knocked at ten doors in every village to research the cooking of the region. I have never met anyone so passionate, so dedicated, so assiduous in the pursuit of traditional recipes, so faithful to their authenticity and protective of their country's heritage as she is.

I first heard of Nevin at the Sheraton Hotel in Istanbul in 1984, when they were introducing a Turkish menu beside their French one, and she had been asked to teach the chefs regional dishes. In no other country is there such a divide between home and restaurant cooking and between the cooking of the city and that of the provinces as there is in Turkey. Restaurants specialise in grilled meats and appetizers. Most professional cooks are the great-grandchildren of the men who cooked at the palace of Topkapı or at the homes of the nobility in Istanbul at the time of the Ottoman Sultans. They come from the same region of Bolu, form a jealously guarded guild which does not allow women even to set foot in a restaurant kitchen, and offer a standard menu of what they call *saray* or palace cooking.

Classic Turkish cooking, which originates in Istanbul, is one of the most widespread and well-known cuisines. In Egypt, when I was a child, the royal family and the ruling elite were of Ottoman origin and their food was our haute cuisine. All the countries which were part of the Ottoman Empire: most of the Arab world and also the Balkans, Hungary, Greece and parts of Russia, adopted the kebabs, pilafs, stuffed vegetables, milk puddings and nutty, syrupy pastries of Istanbul. But an infinitely vast range of dishes from the Anatolian heartland remained unknown even in Istanbul, and it is only in the last fifteen years that some of these regional dishes have started to appear in the city and become immensely popular.

Nevin taught cookery in a girls' technical school, and she herself learnt to cook at the gatherings to which she accompanied her mother around Konya, in the heart of Anatolia, where her father was a carpet dealer. It is part of traditional Turkish life for women to *invite their friends once a month to a great day-long feast where they all join in the cooking, and in Konya there could be twenty such gatherings a month.*

There is a great revival of interest in Turkey in this hidden culinary heritage, and scholars and dieticians are rediscovering the dishes of the countryside and provinces. Much of the activity is focussed in Konya, in central Anatolia, where Nevin's brothers run the Culture and Tourism Association. Since 1979 they have organised an annual food festival which includes a cookery competition, in which mainly peasants and artisans take part, and a scholarly symposium. In 1986 the Association hosted an International Congress in Istanbul, Ankara and Konya. It was a stunning affair with, besides academic papers, a boat trip down the Bosphorus; visits to Topkapı, mosques and museums; a performance by whirling dervishes (Konya is the historic centre of the Mevlevi Order of Dervishes), folk and belly dancing and two banquets a day, including lunch in a private garden where three lambs were cooked in a pit, and dinner in the canteen of a sugar refinery in Konya where local women brought their home-cooked dishes. On that occasion forty-one different dishes were offered, some of which even the Turks among us did not know.

Nevin's book represents a selection of such regional dishes from all over Turkey, with some of the best classics of Istanbul. Her recipes bring back images of the Egyptian spice bazaar of Istanbul – a city within a city with a cupolated roof and hundreds of tiny shops crowded in a warren of lanes and alleys; the specialist tripe soup, milk pudding and pastry makers of Izmir; and all the charm and fascination of Turkey. They make me nostalgic for the incredible warmth and hospitality of the Halıcıs.

Hospitality and gregariousness are deeply entrenched in Turkish life and offering food is what it's all about. "Choose your friend by the taste of his food" is a Turkish proverb which has few equivalents because there are few countries where food is as important as it is in Turkey. Those who have Nevin as a friend count themselves extremely lucky.

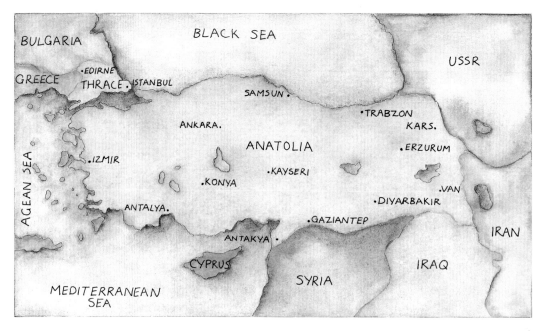

◊ A NOTE ON TURKISH PRONUNCIATION ◊

*Turkish is a phonetic language; all letters are
clearly pronounced, and syllables are
pronounced with more or less equal stress.
Most consonants are pronounced as in English,
but note:*

c as *j* in jam

ç as *ch* in church

g as *g* in gas

ğ is a soft sound, almost silent, which
     lengthens the vowel it follows

h is always pronounced

j occurs in a few foreign words and is
     pronounced as *s* in pleasure

ş as *sh* in ship

The vowel sounds are as follows:

a as *a* in apple

e as *e* in end

ı written without a dot; a sound rather like
     'uh' or *e* in wanted

i as *i* in bill

o as *o* in open

ö not an English sound, but something
     like *ur* in churn

u as *u* in pull

ü like French *u* in tu or German *ü* in
     über

◊ INTRODUCTION ◊

"Heaven and earth are but an apple grown on God's Tree of Infinite Power."
MEVLANA JALALUDDIN-I RUMI, (1207–73).
MESNEVI (POEMS), VOL IV

Great empires have created great cuisines, and the fertile land and the skill of the farmers and fishermen of the Turkish empire have combined with the enthusiasm and abilities of its chefs and home cooks to produce fine, tasty dishes that have ensured a place for Turkish food alongside French and Chinese as one of the three foremost examples of the culinary art in the world.

During the course of its evolution from the Turkish tribes of Central Asia to the present day, Turkish cuisine has acquired an individual character which is expressed in the layout of the kitchen, the cooking utensils, the range of dishes and cooking methods, the presentation of food and serving customs. Every branch of cookery is treated as equally deserving of being rich in variety and succulence.

◊ THE HISTORICAL ◊ EVOLUTION OF TURKISH CUISINE

The history of Turkish cuisine can be considered in its Central Asian, Seljuk and Ottoman periods:

THE CENTRAL ASIAN PERIOD (BEFORE 1038)

Knowledge about the food and eating habits of the early nomad Turks in Central Asia is rather limited and based on conjecture. It is likely that in common with other nomad tribes, they relied on mutton and horse meat, unleavened pastry or bread made of wheat flour, milk and milk products such as yoghurt. Koumiss, a fermented liquor made from mare's milk, and ayran are known to have been drunk.

Evidence from communities of Kazan Turks and Tatars in Anatolia, who still observe many Central Asian customs, indicates that a number of foods from the Central Asian period survive today. Mantı (a kind of ravioli), çörek (ring-shaped buns), various pies and tarhana (a kind of dried curds), all originated in Central Asia.

One of the earliest written sources on pre-Islamic Turks, the Turcic inscriptions of the Orhun Relics, refers to a funeral ceremony of a ruler of the Göktürks, who established a large empire in Central Asia between the sixth and eighth centuries. It shows that deer and hare were the principal meats of these hunters.

THE SELJUK AND PRINCIPALITIES PERIOD (1038–1299)

From the time of the Seljuk sultans more written information about food has sur-

vived. The *Divanu Lugat-i Turk*, a dictionary compiled by Kaşgarlı Mahmut in 1072–3 to teach Turkish to the Arabs, not only gives the names of certain foods, but also describes some dishes. Among those described as old Turkish dishes are tutmaç – noodle soup; yufka – flat unleavened bread; katma juga or katmer – layered pastry; ekmek – bread; yoghurt; ayran; kımız; koumiss; çörek – a ring-shaped bun; pekmez – a syrup made of boiled grape juice; and kavut helva, made with cornflour. There are also references to cooking in a pit dug in the earth, to grills and skewers and earthenware cooking pots.

The other important written work of the 11th century, by Yusuf Has Hacip, entitled *Kutadgu Bilig, The Book of Knowledge*, deals with eating habits, feasts and table service rather than dishes.

Another work which throws light on the same period is the *Dede Korkut Hikayeleri, The Tales of Dede Korkut*, compiled towards the end of the 14th century. These twelve tales are a rich source of information about the customs of the Oghuz Turks who lived in southwestern Asia. Stew (yahni); food on skewers (kebabs); a soup made of wheat flour and yoghurt called togya çorbası in Anatolia; clotted cream; yoghurt; cheese; beverages like milk, ayran, koumiss and wine were all consumed in *The Tales of Dede Korkut*.

The literary works of Mevlana Jalaluddin-i Rumi, who lived in the 13th century, contain many references to the food culture of the time. Mevlana, who conceived the philosophy of harmony and co-operation which can unite people in a crucible of love, provides invaluable knowledge on the subject of food.

Many dishes are categorized and described in detail in Mevlana's works: for example meat is stewed with vegetables which may themselves first be stewed or fried; helva may be made with grape syrup (pekmez helvası) or with almonds (badem helvası); desserts include sweetened boiled rice with saffron (zerde) and starch puddings (paluze).

Mevlana's writings show that in 13th-century Anatolia the following foods and beverages were common: vegetables such as leeks, aubergines, marrows, celeriac, spinach, turnips, onions, garlic, cucumbers; pulses such as blackeyed beans, lentils, chickpeas, broad beans; fruits such as apples, quinces, pomegranates, pears, peaches, figs, melons, watermelons, dates; nuts such as walnuts, almonds, hazelnuts; milk products such as yoghurt, ayran, cheese; food made with flour such as tutmaç – homemade noodles cooked with meat and yoghurt; yufka – flatbread; etli ekmek – flat pastry baked with ground meat; börek – pies; çörek – ring-shaped buns; tırıt – bread cooked in gravy; sweet foods like honey, grapes and grape syrup, helva, kadayif, zerde; drinks such as sweetened fruit juices and wine.

The Mevlevi Order, of whirling dervishes fame, which was founded following the death of Mevlana, established certain rules governing the organization of the kitchen and table manners which are adhered to to this day.

In the Mevlevi Order the kitchen is regarded as a sacred hearth, a temple wherein an inexperienced novice matures and becomes accomplished. The kitchen range, which is the domain of the Ateş Baz-ı Veli – the Guardian Master Cook, can be looked upon as the altar of this temple. The Aşçı Dede – the Sheikh Cook – educates the novices in every respect. The Kazancı Dede – the Sheikh Stoker – is his assistant. An

applicant, before becoming apprenticed in a job in the Order, would sit on a sheepskin in an alcove large enough to accommodate one person only, situated immediately to the left of the entrance to the monastery kitchen. From there he would observe for three days the work, behaviour and actions of the disciples assigned to kitchen duties. He would then make up his mind. If he entered the Order, his noviciate would require spending countless days in the kitchen. The heart of the Mevlevi Order beats in the kitchen. The novices shed their personality in the kitchen and give up all sense of pride. In the kitchen they are taught the rules of conduct and work practice. The Master Cook is their head teacher.

Eighteen different duties are performed in the kitchen:

1 The Sheikh Stoker is the Sheikh Cook's deputy and as a Superior of the Monastery he is responsible for the administration of the kitchen and the novices.

2 The Halife Dede – the Assistant Sheikh – trains the newly admitted novices and shows them how to conduct themselves.

3 The Dervish in charge of External Housework conveys to the dervishes in retreat the orders of the Sheikh Cook.

4 The Laundryman sees to the washing of the habits of the Sheikhs and disciples.

5 The Sanitary Cleaner is in charge of sanitation.

6 The Sherbet Maker makes and serves sherbet to the Sheikhs and the disciples who have ended their noviciate.

7 The Dishwasher washes the kitchen crockery and utensils.

8 The Storekeeper oversees the kitchen equipment and acts as tinsmith.

9 The Stores Purchaser is responsible for buying the food and beverages from the market.

10 The Waiter lays and clears the refectory tables for the Sheikhs and disciples.

11 The Dervish in charge of Internal Housework makes the coffee for the Sheikhs and disciples.

12 The Internal Lamps Attendant lights and maintains the oil lamps in the kitchen.

13 The Coffee Master roasts and grinds the coffee.

14 The Bed Maker makes the beds and changes the linen.

15 The External Lamps Attendant lights and maintains the oil lamps in the courtyard.

16 The Sweeper cleans the kitchen and the courtyard.

17 The Candle Attendant lights and attends to the candles.

18 The Footman runs errands.

Mevlana's cook, Ateş Baz-ı Veli, the Guardian Master Cook, was a prominent personality, about whom the following tale is told. One day Ateş Baz-ı Veli told Mevlana: "There is no more wood to light the cooking range," and Mevlana responded by telling him to place his feet in the range. "All right," said Ateş Baz-ı Veli and he proceeded to stretch his legs and put his feet in the range. The flame which burst from his big toes instantly started the cooking pot boiling. However, as doubt crept into his mind that he might suffer burns, his left big toe scorched. Mevlana was informed of what had happened. He came along and sorrowfully remarked: "How could you Ateş Baz?", implying how could he have entertained any doubt. And the cook placed the big toe of his right foot over his scorched left big toe to conceal it in shame.

Ateş Baz-ı Veli, who died in the year 1285, was buried in a mausoleum of red stone, the first cook to have a mausoleum built in his memory in Turkey. It is revealing of the attention devoted to food and the culinary art and the esteem in which a cook was held during that period.

There is a widely held belief in Turkey today that to visit the mausoleum of Ateş Baz-ı Veli and take away a pinch of salt distributed there, will bring a blessing to the visitors' kitchen, enhance their cooking and prove beneficial for any illness they may suffer from.

The Seljuk archives are an invaluable source of information on the period. When the Seljuk ruler Alaaddin Keykubat I (1227–37) arrived for the first time as a monarch in Konya, the capital of the Seljuk empire, there were fireworks and ceremonies the like of which had never been witnessed before, and feasts and drinking parties were organized. In H. T. H. Houtsma's edition of the Seljuk archives, these feasts are described as follows: "Various kinds of rice and stewed marrow dishes, stewed and fried vegetables, meat stews, unpeeled vegetables cooked in hot ashes, roasts, grilled chickens, pigeons, partridges and quail, all in gold and china dishes, were arranged on a dais in keeping with the traditions of the two clans of the Oghuz Turkish tribes. Koumiss and a variety of sweetened fruit juices were drunk in accordance with Oghuz customs."

There were many organizations in Anatolia at that time which adhered strictly to the regulations and statutes governing the running of kitchens. Foremost among them were the Wakif societies, religious charitable trusts and foundations which provided many free benefits and services.

For example, The Germiyan Oğlu Beyi Yakup Bey soup kitchen in Kütahya provided for its members and for travellers seeking shelter: two meals and four loaves of bread each day; a meat dish each day (both dish and bread had to be excellent); rice and wheat soup; meat, rice and vegetables like spinach and turnips; helva made of flour, butter and sugar and sweet pastry with honey.

For those who arrived too late for meals there was butter, cheese and unleavened flatbread.

In other establishments of this kind guests were offered hospitality for three days according to custom, but here those who wished could extend their stay for longer.

THE OTTOMAN PERIOD
(1299–1923)

During the Ottoman period Turkish cooking became increasingly sophisticated. In the kitchens of the palace and in the homes of the nobles and officials, cooks developed high levels of specialization, and so Istanbul cooking or palace cooking, which is regarded as the pinnacle of Turkish cuisine, was created.

When Sultan Mehmet II, the Conqueror, captured Constantinople in 1453 he ordered as his first act the building of a palace where he could reside. In a famous imperial decree he laid down the conventions to be followed at the court, the rules of protocol to be observed and the table manners to be adhered to in the Topkapı Palace (completed in 1478). The manner in which food was to be prepared and served for the sovereign, his ministers, the court treasury dignitaries and other members of the palace staff was set out.

At the time of Mehmet II the palace kitchen complex comprised four main areas, of which the most important was the Kuşhane – the bird cage kitchen, named after a small cooking pot. In this kitchen only food for the sovereign was prepared in small quantities and in small vessels. The second kitchen, known as the Has Mutfak – the sovereign's kitchen, was where food destined for the mother of the sultan, the princes and the privileged members of the harem was prepared. The other kitchens included the kitchens of the harem, the chief eunuch, the imperial state chancery and members of the palace household according to their ranks.

The member of the household responsible for the kitchens was the head butler and he, with the chefs who headed the kitchen and the kitchen superintendent, who was responsible for materials and provisions, formed the triumvirate of personnel who ran the kitchen.

During the reign of Mehmet II the kitchen staff included bakers, dessert cooks, helva makers, pickle makers, the chief yoghurt maker etc. The move towards culinary specialization already witnessed in the Mevlevi monastery in the 13th century had been accomplished by the 15th. The entire staff in the palace kitchens strove to produce dishes that were exquisite, and experimented with new ideas to improve existing dishes.

dishes and admired the service and the table-ware, although he wondered why the dried fruit compote (hoşaf) which followed the rice dish had not been served in as attractive a bowl as the rest. The mufti explained that in order not to spoil the texture of the fruit, he did not allow chips of ice to be added to it, but instead had the juice frozen in a mould fashioned like a bowl and served the compote in that.

Just as in the palace kitchens, all Ottoman grand houses employed staff who specialized in particular aspects of the culinary art.

At this period various chefs' guilds were organized in the capital and to this day they continue to play an important role in perpetuating and improving old recipes. Under Ottoman rule only the best ingredients were brought into Istanbul, and the sale of inferior foods was prevented under a system of very strict control. This fact, together with the lively competition between cooks and confectioners to provide the best, ensured that high standards were always maintained.

Among the various confectioners who have been carrying on their trade since time immemorial in Istanbul, the muhallebiciler, the makers and sellers of milk dishes are unique. Even though rare these days, one can still come across their shops in Istanbul selling chicken soup, rice cooked with chicken, tavuk göğsü – blancmange with thin strips of breast of chicken (p.148), and similar milk dishes and light desserts.

Here we must also mention the street traders, who, in the Istanbul of bygone days used to make and sell special kinds of food. There was the çörekçi – maker of sweet buns; börekçi – of savoury pastries; simitçi – of bread rolls; kağit helvacı – of pastry wafers with sweetmeat; poğaçacı – of various kinds of pies; the lokmacı – fritter maker; gözlemeci – pancake maker; lokum ve şekerlemeci – lokum (Turkish delight)

The nobles and officials entertained each other regularly and competed to provide the best food. Those who boasted kitchens of the same excellence as the palace kitchens saw their fame spread, and the sultans honoured them by paying them a visit. Thus, during the reign of Sultan Mehmet II, the Grand Mufti Abdullah Molla (the head of the Islamic establishment who ranked second to the Grand Vizier, the head of government) became famous for his generosity, wealth, nobility and cuisine. One evening, at the time of breaking the fast during Ramadan, the sultan gathered his ministers and paid an unannounced visit to the mufti's residence. The butler, finding himself face to face with the sultan, hurried excitedly to his master. The mufti urged the butler not to panic and told him to serve the sultan with his own meal and to give the other guests two or three trays of food reserved for the harem. After the meal the sultan remarked on the succulence of the

and sweet maker; helvacı – helva maker; kelle-paçacı – maker of sheep's head and trotters soup; pilavcı – of rice dishes; köfteci – of meatballs – and so on. In my opinion the most original of them all were the ones who plied their trade in boats selling fried fish. In the past these traders used to fish in Istanbul's clean sea, prepare and wash in sea water the freshly caught fish, and after dipping them in flour, fry them in oil on charcoal stoves in their boats, put them with chopped onions in half a loaf of bread sliced through the middle and sell them. For passengers waiting to depart on ships and ferries moored along the quay or the crowds on the shore, it was a pleasure to buy fish from these boats and to eat them. One or two such boats still survive.

Turkish cuisine owes its development and survival to this day to the practical culinary expertise which the palace, the grand houses and the numerous associations of cooks and confectioners passed on from generation to generation. The Turkish saying "Never mind what you ate and drank, tell me where you have been and what you have seen", shows it was considered bad manners to talk about food and this is why there is little culinary literature in Turkish.

Apart from some dictionaries and medical books based on early studies which gave descriptions of dishes or definitions of foodstuffs, the first cookery book was a translated work entitled *Tabh-i Et'ime – Instruction in Cookery*, believed to have been translated from the Arabic *Kitabut-Tabih – The Book of Cookery* in the 15th century by Şirvani. Other noteworthy books are *Ağıdiye Risalesi – The Manual of Nourishment* by Abdullah Efendi, and *Yemek Risalesi – A Manual of Dishes* by unknown authors published in the 18th century. The *Melceu't Tabbahin – The Sanctuary of Cooks*, compiled in 1844 by Mehmet Kamil was the first cookery book to be printed by lithography; it was later translated into English by Turabi Efendi.

The 20th-century books which deserve most attention are *Yemek Kitabı – A Book of Recipes*, and *Tatlıcı Başı – The Dessert Chef*, written in the old Turkish script based on the Arabic alphabet by Hadiye Fahriye and published in 1924 and 1926 respectively. Although by this time some foreign influences could be found in Turkish cookery there is little sign of it in these two works which offer classic Turkish cuisine. However, later cookery books carry many traces of foreign cuisine, and today there is a conscious effort to eliminate these traces and restore Turkish cooking to its origins.

There has undoubtedly been a great deal of cross-fertilization in the development of Turkish food. When the Turks came west from central Asia they borrowed elements from the cookery of the countries they traversed, and also adopted some of the foods of earlier Anatolian civilizations. An important character of Turkish cuisine is its ability to assimilate whatever it has borrowed and produce a successful synthesis.

There are of course several culinary similarities with the food of neighbouring regions which have much the same climate and vegetation. For instance the red cabbage soup of the Black Sea region resembles Russian borscht; some desserts and meatballs made with boiled and pounded wheat are like those of Turkey's southern neighbours; while pilaki dishes of stewed fish or beans served cold have their counterparts in Greek cooking.

Börek – savoury pastries; kebabs; baklava – a pastry dessert with syrup and nuts; yoghurt; lokum – Turkish delight; and Turkish coffee have all spread abroad from Turkey.

Çerkez tavuğu – Circassian chicken (p.40); arnavut ciğeri – Albanian liver (p.77); kürt köftesi – Kurdish meatballs; arap köftesi – Arab meatballs, are examples of foreign foods widely found in Turkish and Anatolian cuisine. These days some adaptations of western dishes are to be seen too.

THE INFLUENCE OF ISLAM IN TURKISH CUISINE AND FORBIDDEN FOODS

Following the conversion of the Turks to Islam in the ninth century, Islamic influences became apparent in Turkish cuisine and indeed in other cultural spheres. As well as introducing the practice of observing certain holy days and eating some foods considered sacred, Islam also brought certain restrictions concerning food and drink. According to the restrictions laid down in the Koran four foods are strictly forbidden in the Islamic world: the meat of animals that have died by means other than having their throats cut; blood from an animal's body; pork; and the meat of an animal slaughtered as a sacrifice in the name of any other than God.

The Koran makes no reference to meat derived from "loathsome" animals: reptiles and beasts of prey, but its consumption is considered harmful by Islamic scholars, although it is not forbidden in canonical terms. Prevalent opinion about the consumption of aquatic animals is that it is canonically lawful. The Koran states: "To fish in the sea and to consume the catch is lawful for you and the travellers as a means of subsistence." Taking the message of this verse one step further, it is considered lawful to eat crustaceans killed by means other than the correct ritual, and also locusts among terrestrial insects.

Although in the Islamic world preference is given to meat from an animal slaughtered by a Moslem, it is permitted to eat meat from animals slaughtered by members of other faiths with their own scriptures.

However, the manner of slaughtering must conform to the Moslem rite, in other words the throat of the animal must be slit.

As to beverages, the Koran forbids alcoholic drinks, but the fact that the Koran uses the term "wine" has led lovers of alcoholic drinks to argue that they are not forbidden. However, the Prophet Mohammed said: "That which causes any form of inebriation is wine and any kind of wine is forbidden."

The restrictions are waived when canonically lawful nourishment to relieve hunger and thirst or to treat an illness are not available. In such circumstances a Moslem may consume what is normally forbidden.

These restrictions apart, Islam brought to Turkish social life and cuisine new customs and rituals, and was responsible for certain foods assuming a sacred significance.

In Islam the month of Ramadan is the month of fasting, observed throughout the country. There are also five Kandil nights – religious feast nights, when the minarets of mosques are illuminated. The dates and months refer to the Arabic Calendar based on the lunar year, which is still used in the Islamic world to determine the dates of religious events. The twelfth night of Rebiü-levvel – the third month – is the Prophet Mohammed's birthday. The first Friday of Receb – the seventh month – is known as Ragaib Kandili, and marks the Prophet Mohamed's conception; that is the night when, it is believed, one's prayers are answered. The 27th night of Receb is known as Mirac Kandili, the night of Prophet Mohammed's ascent to heaven. The 15th night of Şaban – the eighth month – is Berat Gecesi, the Night of Privilege, when the future actions of an individual for the following year are considered, decreed and duly noted by the angels. The night of the 27th of Ramadan – the ninth month – is the Kandil Gecesi, the night of Power, the night the Koran was revealed to the world.

During the day preceding these feasts it is a widely observed tradition throughout Anatolia to make and distribute three sacred foods which, according to popular folklore, represent Mohammed's seal: lokma – fritters; the Prophet's written edict: katmer – flaky pastry; and his blessing: pişi – fried puff pastry.

Aşura, which falls on the 10th of Muharrem – the first month – is a popular feast day. Believing that on this day God granted his nine prophets favours and created the heavens, people celebrate the occasions with great enthusiasm and exchange gifts of aşure – a sweet made of cereals, rice, sugar, fresh and dried fruit and milk (p.152).

THE LAYOUT OF A KITCHEN

In old Turkish houses the kitchen was divided into two sections, the pantry and the kitchen proper. Usually the pantry was located in an area sheltered from the sun and had small windows to provide good ventilation and a door leading into the kitchen.

Goods which had to be stored for a long time were kept in the pantry. Around the pantry walls a step was built some 5–10cm/ 2–3 inches above the ground. On this would rest rows of jars containing oil, preserves, grape syrup, honey, pickles, each jar covered with lacework, and similar foodstuffs grouped together in neat sections. Sucuk – sausages, and pastırma – dried meat seasoned with cumin and garlic – were hung in

muslin bags on hooks on the wall or from wooden poles. Fruit such as grapes, melons and pears to be stored for the winter were also hung up and preserved. Dry goods such as flour, pulses, rice and cracked wheat, were likewise kept in the pantry and taken out as required for daily use in the kitchen.

In the kitchen the range was placed under a chimney hood which drew away unpleasant smells. A basin and a fountain were provided for washing up. Above and to one side of the basin-stand were rows of shelves rising from floor level, the bottom ones wide enough to take frying pans and saucepans, and the upper ones narrower for china. In a convenient place stood a large wire-mesh corner cupboard, which held cooked dishes and daily foodstuffs. Resting on the floor long padded seats and cushions were placed facing each other, which made it possible to work seated when one was preparing vegetables and fruit or rolling out pastry.

The kitchen range apart, two types of braziers were used: the mangal brazier which used charcoal for cooking a wide range of dishes, and the maltız brazier which used coke for cooking dishes needing intense heat such as sheep's head, trotters and tripe. Food that needed cooking in an oven was sent to the local bakery. Kitchens were generally laid out in the same fashion, but sometimes special regional features such as a tandır, a pit dug in the earth and used as an oven in southern Anatolia, would be added.

KITCHEN UTENSILS

The utensils used in the Turkish kitchen can be described according to the material they are made from.

Wooden utensils: the most important utensils in every home are the pastry board, the kneading trough, the circular tambour, a frame or folding trestle that supports the large tray which serves as a meal table, various sizes of rolling pins, spoons used in cooking and for eating, and a spoon container.

Copper utensils: large round trays that serve as a meal table, bowls, drinking vessels, a shallow saucepan with handles, trays, cooking pots, yoghurt and milk buckets, large deep serving dishes, plates, perforated and solid ladles, strainers, frying pans, cleavers, carrying bowls.

Brass utensils: a mortar, coffee grinder, pitchers for salep (the powdered root of *Orchis mascula* mixed with milk as a hot drink in winter) and şerbet (sweetened fruit juice).

Enamel utensils: all sizes of saucepans, coffee jugs, a hot water pot and teapot (designed so that the latter sits on top of the former as a single unit).

Earthenware utensils: various sizes of casseroles with lids, small soup bowls for individual helpings, a fish kettle and tray, pitchers, water jugs, and bowls.

Porcelain ware: dinner service, coffee service, salep service, and crockery.

Glassware: water glasses, şerbet glasses, tea service, dessert plates and bowls.

Other wares: sweetmeat and other dessert moulds, vinegar holder, salt dispenser, meat grilling skewers, griddle, stone and iron mortars.

MEALS AND MANNERS

From the times of the Seljuks to the present day, the Turks generally adopted the habit of having four meals a day, two main meals and two light refreshments.

The first meal is prepared for the time when the family elders depart for work, that is, after morning prayers and some two hours before the midday call to prayers. This meal is known as Kuşluk Yemeği, the literal translation is "aviary meal", signifying small in quantity, like breadcrumbs for birds. At noon, with the menfolk away, food remaining from the previous evening or a light snack serves for lunch.

The second main meal of the day, prepared after the evening prayers, is the dinner, which brings the family together at home. For this meal the best dishes are painstakingly prepared.

The fourth meal of the day, which is eaten just before retiring, especially during the long winter evenings, is known in central Anatolia as Yat Geber Ekmeği – "Hit the Pillow and Drop Dead" – a supper of breakfast foods, fruit, sweetened buns, pastries. It is said the meal got its name because men who stayed out drinking all evening would return home in the middle of the night and beg their wives to produce breakfast or soup to soak up their drinks. The wife, annoyed at her husband, but remaining silent out of respect for him, would mutter to herself: "Take this, hit the pillow and drop dead and don't bother me any more."

These daily meals naturally differed in families particularly keen on food or when guests were invited; then lunch, for instance, would be treated as a main meal.

The following notes appear in the 11th-century *Kutadgu Bilig – The Book of Knowledge*, concerning meals and table manners:

"Let your home, your dining table and your plates be clean. Let your room be furnished with padded cushions and let your food and beverages be freshly made. The food and beverages must be clean and tasty too, to encourage your guests to enjoy their meal. The food and beverages to be consumed during the meal must be complementary and plentiful. The beverages to be offered to the guests must not be lacking in quantity and the accompaniments to each course must always be ready to serve. As beverages, offer either fuka (a sweet juice made of cereal grains and fruit) or mizab (drinking water) – or rose honey and sweetened rose juice. When the meal is over, serve delicacies and fruit. Alongside dried and fresh fruit offer simis (marrow seeds soaked in salt water and then fried) as a delicacy. Finally, if your circumstances permit, present the guests with gifts. If you are wealthy, make a present of silk materials, and if possible end the occasion with a very special gift to render the visitors speechless."

In the 13th century the rules governing table manners in the Mevlevi monastery were as follows:

"When the food was cooked and ready in the kitchen, the Kazan Dede – the Sheikh Stoker – took the lid off the large cooking pot or saucepan and the disciples bowed down to the ground. The Sheikh Stoker recited a prayer; the 'table' was laid in the kitchen and sheepskin rugs were placed all around it. One of the disciples then proceeded to the chambers of the Dervishes and called out: 'The meal is served', and repeated this summons for the benefit of the novices. Around the edge of the large metal tray which served as a table small towels were laid. The spoons were placed facing downwards with the handles pointing to the right. The head of the monastic order, the Head Dervish or the Aşçı Dede – the Sheikh Cook – also sat at the table; all the dervishes and disciples known as Mevlevis took their places at the table. Strict silence was observed during the meal. The meal began with a prayer, and by tasting a pinch of salt taken from the salt cellar placed on the table; likewise a pinch of salt was

taken at the end of the meal and the meal ended with a prayer. The disciples whose duty it was to serve water prepared the pitchers, and after filling the tumbler of the individual who has signalled his need for water, the disciple concerned lifted the tumbler, kissed it and handed it back. The individual receiving the tumbler also kissed it and then drank the water. During the performance of this rite, those seated at the table refrained from helping themselves to food and from eating, and those with food in their mouths stopped chewing. The Sheikh Cook then addressed the individual who drank the water with the words 'well done' and those assembled resumed eating. The meal was eaten from a common serving dish. With the thought that 'the leftovers of a believer are beneficial to another believer' each course was finished up. After the end-of-meal prayer and grace had been said, the disciples – Mevlevis – and the Dervishes left the table in silence in an atmosphere of piety."

Today in traditional homes, particularly in the Anatolian countryside, these customs still persist, and meals are served in the old manner on the floor. Everyone washes his hands and takes a place at the table. The elder of the family starts the meal after saying grace. Everyone helps himself from a large common serving dish placed in the middle. For soup, rice and stewed fruit spoons are used. Other dishes are eaten by hand, though nowadays forks are also used. If someone leaves the table no-one touches the food until that person returns. When the meal is over, grace is said and the elders leave the table first.

Certain practices have to be observed in eating food by hand. Meatballs, grilled or roasted meat, stuffed vegetables and so on are picked up by one end and eaten. Dishes in gravy or sauce must be eaten without dipping one's fingers in the juice. Usually

such dishes are eaten with bread. (Bread is the Turk's staple food and everything else is considered as supplementary.) The thumb, index and middle fingers are used to pick up the food. The piece of vegetable or meat nearest to the edge of the common serving dish is pulled to the very edge with a piece of bread held between index and middle finger. Then the morsel of food is grasped from underneath with the thumb (often this is not necessary as soft food such as helva would stick to the bread) and lifted to the mouth. Meat on the bone is eaten by holding one end of the bone. Wet flannels sprinkled with rosewater are provided and used at intervals to wipe the hands and mouth.

When the meal is over an end-of-meal prayer is said. If time is pressing, the shorter form of prayer is said with the words "In the name of God, thanks be to God, glory be to God". Then the final morsel of food is taken and it is customary to pick this last morsel from the furthest part of the serving dish. (It is believed that by doing so one is reunited in spirit with friends and relatives who are away from home.) Then everyone leaves the table and once hands are washed, coffee is served.

TABLE SETTING AND SERVICE

The Turks of Central Asia used to take their meals on a linen or leather "ground sheet" called a kenduruk, which was spread out on the floor, whereas in the 11th century they used a tergi or tewsi – a large tray.

In those days Turkish architecture did not provide for a separate dining room in the home; at meal times a table was laid in the main room and food was served there. Even at the Topkapı Palace residence of the Otto-man sultans there is no separate dining hall and meals were served on dining tables laid in different parts of the palace.

Today a traditional Turkish meal table is laid on the floor as follows: first of all a "table-cloth" is spread on the floor to prevent bread and food from soiling the floor. On it is placed a large tray resting upon a tambour, a circular frame, or a trestle so as to raise it to the correct height. A wooden soup spoon for each person is laid either around the soup tureen or around the edge of the table according to personal preference. If indivi-dual napkins are provided, these are placed on the spoons; if not, one long napkin cloth is laid, stretching all round the table. Tum-blers, water jugs, dishes of food and des-serts are placed on a smaller tray close by.

Small hand towels soaked in hot soapy water and sprinkled with toilet water, usu-ally rosewater, are provided to wipe the hands now and again.

Before starting the meal, a hand-washing bowl and a jug of water are brought in and hands are washed, beginning with the chil-dren, then everyone sits down to eat.

The meal begins with the soup tureen being placed in the middle of the table, and then the mother or the daughter of the household, if there is no servant, brings in the dishes, collects the empty plates and serves the next course. Ayran – a yoghurt drink; şerbet – sweetened fruit juices; surup – syrups; and salads and pickles are placed on the table as additional delicacies. When the dessert or stewed fruit is served, special dessert spoons are handed round. If little children are present, a separate small serving dish might be placed on the table for their benefit.

When the meal is over the table is cleared, once again the hand-washing bowl is brought in and hands are washed, the elders first this time. Then coffee, and tobacco for the men, are offered.

MENUS AND MEALS FOR SPECIAL OCCASIONS

The first recorded banquet is Yuğ, the mourning feast to be seen on the Orhun relics. In the 11th century, during religious holidays or for the marriages of a khan, banquet meals, known as Kenc Liyu, were stacked in the form of a minaret, rising to a height of 30 arşın (an archaic Turkish measure equalling approximately 70cm/28 inches) for the public to demolish and consume.

In the same century Yusuf Has Hacip had the following to say about arranging menus and the rules to be followed at a banqueting table: "If too great a heat is felt as a result of eating too many hot dishes, immediately drink something cold. If you are in the springtime of your life, then show preference for colder things, for your blood will warm them up. If you are over 40 years of age and in the autumn of your life, regulate your disposition with hot things. If you are 60 years of age and in your winter, eat hot things and do not flirt with cold things. If you have consumed too many dry and cold

foods, keep hot and fresh things in readiness (in order to avoid their detrimental effects). If you feel your old age and the cold too much, fortify yourself with heat. If you have a hot temperament, nurture yourself with cold things. If you wish to be always healthy and never to suffer from indisposition, eat in moderation and live by this rule. If you wish to enjoy a long life in complete peace of mind, then be quiet and hold your tongue, and live by this rule, ye pure-hearted being.

"Do not start to eat before your elders. Always begin your meal by saying grace and eat with your right hand. Do not touch the food in front of another person, and eat what is nearest to you. Do not produce a knife at the table and do not strip a bone clean, do not be too voracious and do not slouch. But, however sated you might feel, show pleasure and keenness in accepting the food that is offered to you and in consuming it so that the lady of the house, who prepared the dishes, can be pleased. In this way render worthwhile the effort of those who took the trouble of entertaining you to a meal. Bite what you put into your mouth and chew it slowly. Do not blow with your mouth over hot food. When you are eating do not slouch over the table and do not disturb the people next to you. Eat in a measured manner, for a person should always eat and drink little."

A Turkish meal is generally composed of soup, a main course of meat, rice or stuffed savoury pastry, a vegetable dish and a dessert, and provides as much variety as possible within that sequence.

Banqueting menus exist offering a selection of up to 100 dishes for banquets at the palace in Istanbul and up to 40 dishes in Anatolia. Nowadays a formal set menu is likely to consist of soup, an egg dish, fish, meat, poultry or game, vegetables cooked with fat or olive oil, börek (stuffed savoury pastry), pilaf or pasta, desserts, fruit and coffee.

In a 16th-century work entitled *Banqueting Arrangements*, it is suggested that a drinks supper table should be decorated with flowers and sprinkled with rose petals. Essential at such a function were roasts cooked rare, sour-flavoured soups, fried food, meatballs; various kinds of fish and shellfish were served as meze or hors d'oeuvres. It recommends providing at least 40 or 50 different items in the meze and that hazelnuts, pistachios and almonds should be plentiful; that the table should be over-flowing with fish roe, caviar and various kinds of pastırma (dried meat seasoned with cumin and garlic) and that except for rice, heavy foods such as stuffed pastry and the like should be avoided.

It is said that in later years drinks suppers with roughly the same variety of food were provided at various taverns in Istanbul and that the district of Yedi Kule – Seven Towers – acquired a reputation especially for its mezes. Today the locality is known as Çiçek Pasajı – Flower Alley – in Istanbul; it is famous for its drinks and mezes.

At drinks parties now the cold dishes are laid out on the table and hot dishes are brought in in turn and served. Tripe soup is the customary end to an evening of this kind.

Another special supper, which survives in a few homes in Anatolia, is the helva supper. Helva suppers originated in Istanbul in the homes of the well-connected headed by Ibrahim Pasha and his sons-in-law during the reign of Sultan Ahmet III (1703–30, the Tulip Period). Helva was served following sessions of discussion and various forms of entertainment. Sultan Ahmet III used to attend many of these helva gatherings.

In Turkish cuisine there is a special place for the Sahur and Iftar meals, the meals taken before and at the end of the daily period of abstinence during the religious month of fasting.

Fasting during the month of Ramadan, which is one of the five essential require-ments of Islam, is an act of piety under-taken by going without food or drink from about an hour before the morning prayer until the call to evening prayer. In the olden days in Istanbul, Ramadan was greeted in a festive atmosphere and it livened up social life. Illuminations strung up between mina-rets were all lit up, the hours of Iftar and Sahur were heralded with the beating of drums and the firing of a cannon; through-out the month entertainments and games were organized at Direklerarası Amuse-ment Park. In preparation homes were smartened up a month ahead, stocks of foodstuffs were topped up, some of the food purchased for Ramadan in grand houses was donated to the widows and poor ladies of families of the district.

The Iftar meal was prepared before the call to evening prayer. Before the Iftar meal the fast was broken by first taking breakfast in order not to fill an empty stomach with rich and heavy food. Having breakfasted, evening prayer was said (some well-to-do families acquired the services of an Imam for the duration of Ramadan), and there-after everyone gathered together for the Iftar meal.

On the breakfast tray which served as a table there appeared various jams, honey, cheese, caviar, olives, sausages, pastırma – all especially prepared for Ramadan. Alongside these would be fresh fruit, salads, cups of blessed water, dates and mustard. Small plates bearing lemons cut in half and wrapped in muslin and tied with coloured ribbons were conveniently placed on the table to serve both as a decoration and as receptacles for depositing fruit stones. White bread; pide – slightly leavened flat-

bread; çörek – ring-shaped sweetened buns; simit – ring-shaped bread, completed the breakfast fare.

The Iftar meal always ended with dried fruit compote. The special dessert for Ramadan known as güllaç – starch wafers filled with nuts, and milky syrup flavoured with rosewater – made repeat appearances on the menu every two or three days.

The people of Istanbul used to be particularly keen on tripe soup – işkembe çorbası. As the time for breaking the fast approached, queues formed in front of the premises of tripe soup sellers. If an Iftar banquet or dinner was being given, then gifts were presented at the end as customary at all banquets or formal dinners. In some houses in Istanbul a tiny gold nugget fashioned in the shape of a chickpea was inserted in a dish of rice and chickpeas for a lucky winner to find. The person in whose spoon the gold chickpea was discovered received the principal gift.

After the Iftar meal came the superogatory night prayers and then everyone proceeded to the entertainment parks where until Sahur they were entertained with concerts of string music, theatrical performances, karagöz – the Turkish shadow-show, puppet shows and story tellers.

Sahur meals were made up of lighter dishes because after a heavy meal one felt rather satiated. Moreover, a heavy meal might cause thirst. The Sahur meal of a middle-class family consisted of dishes such as minced meat wrapped in vine leaves, macaroni with minced meat or cheese, meatballs and fruit compote.

These days the Iftar and Sahur meals are much the same, but without the gift heralded by the discovery of a gold chickpea! The custom of friends and relatives entertaining each other to meals during Ramadan continues.

TURKISH CUISINE AND THE REGIONAL DIFFERENCES OF OUR DAY

Turkish cooking today covers classic Turkish cuisine, or palace cuisine, which evolved in Istanbul from the imperial palace, noble homes and chefs' guilds, and which today is practised only in private homes; international cuisine, largely served in tourist restaurants and hotels; and popular Turkish cuisine which thrives in Anatolian dishes based on regional produce. Many of these dishes, although described in old documents, were unknown in Istanbul and never incorporated into the classic repertoire.

Ekmek dolmasi, a loaf of bread stuffed with meat and cooked in a bain-marie, and haşhaşli çörek (p.165) – ring-shaped poppy seed cakes, come from the Aegean region; saksuka – vegetable stew with aubergines, peppers, potatoes, tomatoes and garlic; and kabak helvası – a dessert made with marrow, are from the Mediterranean region; maş piyazi – a dish of mung beans and onions (p.116); and külünce – a highly spiced pastry (p.160), are from southeastern Anatolia; keledos – a dish of pulses, vegetables and meat; and mirtoğa – a spicy sweetish cheese (p.43), are from eastern Anatolia; hamsi pilavi – a dish of rice and anchovies; and lahana çorbasi – red cabbage soup, are from the Black Sea region; çebiç – lamb cooked on a spit; and arabasi – chicken and vegetable soup, are from central Anatolia; none of these dishes are found in Istanbul cuisine and all of them are based on the produce of the region.

Now a comprehensive study of popular Turkish cuisine is underway, and work on recipes recorded in archives has been attracting attention in recent years. When these recipes, many of which date back to the earliest history of the Turks, are brought to light, and recipes of present day and recent Anatolian dishes are properly recorded, and all this material is looked at together with the recipes of Istanbul cuisine, the true characteristics of Turkish cooking will emerge and it will then be possible to appreciate it in its entirety.

Now let us consider the regional features of Turkish cooking. Anatolia is made up of seven geographic regions: the Marmara region takes in the centre of Turkish cuisine – Istanbul. This region is well known for the sunflower oil produced in its most western part, Thrace (European Turkey), and for the cheese of Edirne. The Anatolian part is particularly rich in vegetables and fruit. Bursa is the town which gave birth, as it were, to the döner kebab – meat roasted on a revolving vertical spit, and Bolu is the town from which came the most famous cooks of Ottoman days, and many of the best chefs still come from there.

The Aegean region is renowned for its fish and seafood: the produce of the southern part which stretches down the coast from Izmir is the most sought-after in Turkey, and there is a great variety of leaf vegetable dishes.

The Mediterranean region, despite being a coastal region, does not have a great variety of fish and consequently of fish dishes; this is probably due to over-fishing and pollution. The western part bordering on the lower end of the Aegean region is much richer in produce. The eastern part, like the neighbouring region of southeastern Anatolia, is well known for its acılı kebab – meat roasted with hot peppers, and bulgurlu köfte – meatballs with boiled and pounded wheat. Adana kebab and şalgam suyu – turnip juice, also deserve attention.

Southeastern Anatolia offers the best examples of the Turkish range of roast meats, an art in itself. The town of Gaziantep probably has the widest range of meat dishes and also has excellent baklava – a diamond-shaped sweet pastry made with pistachio nuts and produced here on a commercial scale. Çiğ köfte – spiced raw meatballs (p.71) and peynirli kadayıf – sweet pastry made with cheese, are the specialities of Şanli Urfa. Künefe is one of the noteworthy dishes of Antakya (the ancient town of Antioch). The town of Diyarbakır has a rich array of traditional dishes, including bumbar – a kind of sausage, kelle-paça – sheep's head and trotter soup (p.75), kaburga dolmasi – stuffed breast of kid (p.58), all found in restaurants. And a favourite at home is a delicious dessert called nuriye, a wafery sweet pastry filled with nuts and milky syrup.

Eastern Anatolia, which has a cold climate, is the region of grain and cereal production and livestock farming. Butter, yoghurt, ayran, cheese, honey, cereals and pulses shape the character of the local cooking.

Ayran soup, keledos – a dish of beans, meat and vegetables, and kurt köftesi – meatballs, are famed specialities. Dishes prepared with yoghurt are flavoured with the aromatic herbs to be found in the mountains of the region. Tea, of course, is the region's legendary beverage, so much so that in the villages, even in quite poor families, they still employ a "tea-minder" in the home who keeps everyone supplied with tea at all times. Butter and honey from Kars, the delicious cheese known as sirmo ve mendu from Van, prepared with herbs picked on the mountains during the months of April and May and matured in earthenware jars buried upside down in theground; from Erzincan cheese in a goatskin container known as tomast, so good one can never get enough of it: these are the foods to taste in the region.

The mere mention of the Black Sea region immediately brings to mind food prepared with fish and especially anchovies. There are at least 40 different anchovy dishes, and many ballads, poems and anecdotes written about anchovies! The second thing for which this region is famous is maize flour and dishes made with it, such as kaymak. Green and red cabbage are popular here, and hamsiköy sütlacı (literally "anchovy village rice pudding") – a savoury dish – is a dish with a reputation that extends beyond the regional border. The region is most renowned for tea cultivated in the Rize area.

Central Anatolia has developed an excellent cuisine by virtue of the fact that, alongside cereal cultivation and livestock rearing, it produces all kinds of fruit and vegetables. Konya, which was the capital of the Seljuk Turks, has achieved distinction in terms of both its food industry and its domestic cooking. Spurred on by the same competitive spirit and desire to produce the best which prevailed in the grand houses of Istanbul, Konya's home cooking offers examples of excellence and richness the like of which I have not encountered anywhere else. Etli ekmek – bread cooked with meat, peynirli pide – flat leavened bread cooked with cheese, and fırın kebabı – a particular way of roasting meat, are dishes which are constantly praised.

Other noteworthy dishes of the region include Ankara tavası – an Ankara dish made with chickpeas, grapes, nuts and meat boiled and then cooked in the oven; pastırma – dried meat seasoned with cumin and garlic, and mantı – stuffed pasta (p.134), all specialities of Kayseri (ancient Caeserea).

COOKING METHODS

Cooking methods can be considered under four broad headings:

1 COOKING WITH WATER

Many foods are boiled and some are then finished by another method. Steaming is little used nowadays except for dishes like mussels stuffed with rice. It is said that in the past rice was cooked without direct contact with water, the prepared rice being put in a small pot which in turn was placed in a large cooking pot filled with water.

2 FRYING IN OIL

Both deep- and shallow-frying are used for fritters, croquettes, meatballs, etc.

3 COOKING BY DRY HEAT

Many foods – meat, pastries, vegetables – are baked in the oven. A gridiron, the oldest means of cooking in Turkey, is still used extensively for cooking bread, stuffed savoury pastries, meats etc., over an open fire.

Another age-old method is to cook fruits and vegetables with firm skins in the embers of a charcoal fire. The baked vegetables are either cut in half and buttered, or peeled and used in other dishes such as puréed aubergine (hünkar beğendi) or (ali nazik, p.64).

Grilling over embers is also very common. Meat or fish cooked over a charcoal fire, cannot be compared for taste with those cooked by gas or electricity. In addition to grilling over an open fire, there is another way of broiling meat – to put the meat in a container and bury it in a fire made in a pit dug in the earth. See çebiç (p.60).

4 COOKING WITH FAT AND WATER

This is the most common cooking method. It covers all kinds of stews and casseroles which are classified in categories such as yahni – stewed meat or fish; basti – vegetable ragouts; oturtma – dishes of minced meat with vegetables, dolma – stuffed vegetables, and pilaf – rice dishes.

SERVINGS

The amount of food per person in the recipes is based on the assumption that a five-course Turkish menu is planned, consisting of soup, a meat dish, a börek, a vegetable dish and dessert. If the menu consists of fewer courses, the quantity per person may be increased.

In the case of dishes such as baklava, börek etc., which cannot be made in small quantities, the recipes are for larger numbers.

◊

SOUPS, APPETIZERS
AND EGGS

◊

◊ ÇORBALAR ◊

S O U P S

*I*n classical Turkish cuisine a meal always starts with soup. It is said that Turks in Central Asia drank tarhana soup – a soup of dried curds and cereals – and the 11th-century Classical Turkish Dictionary has an entry for tutmaç soup made with noodles, meat and yoghurt.

Turkish soups are generally served hot, even in the hotter regions, but there are exceptions, and in Adıyaman in southeastern Anatolia döğmeli yoğurt çorbası – a soup made with yoghurt – is served cold. In Mardin this same soup is served cold as a dessert with grape syrup (pekmez) poured on it. The Easter lunch menu of the Christian inhabitants of Mardin, composed of roast mutton, rice, boiled eggs and Easter cakes, also includes this cold soup which they believe represents the purity of the Virgin Mary.

Until 50 or 60 years ago, soup was drunk in Turkey from wooden spoons to minimize the danger of scalding one's mouth.

◊ TANDIR ÇORBASI ◊

P I T   O V E N   S O U P

*I*n Konya tandır soup is always made on baking day. It is named after the pit oven (p.60) in which it is cooked. All the ingredients are placed raw in an earthenware cooking pot, the lid is put on and sealed with a flour and water paste. Then the casserole is lowered into the hot cinders that remain in the pit oven after bread has been baked early in the day, and the soup cooks in time for a midday meal.

The discovery at the Çatalhöyük archaeological site, not far from Konya, of lentils and bulgur (cracked wheat) and of ovens similar to the tandır indicates that the ancestor of this dish was eaten in Konya 7–8,000 years ago.

TO SERVE 6
50g/2oz minced meat
50g/2oz fat
50g/2oz onions, finely chopped
25g/1oz tomato purée
50g/2oz lentils, soaked overnight
25g/1oz chickpeas, soaked overnight
25g/1oz haricot beans, soaked overnight
50g/2oz bulgur
1.5L/2½ pints meat stock
1tsp red pepper
½tsp ground black pepper
½tsp dried mint
salt as necessary

Put the minced meat, fat and onions in a pan, and fry for 4–5 minutes stirring occasionally. Add the tomato purée and stir for a minute. Add the lentils, chickpeas, haricot beans and bulgur. Pour on the stock, then stir in the red and black pepper and the mint, cover, bring to the boil, and reduce the heat. Cook for 2½–3 hours until the beans and chickpeas are tender. Add salt, cook for another 10 minutes, then serve hot in the cooking pan.

◊ TARHANA ÇORBASI ◊

TARHANA SOUP

Tarhana soup has long been a favourite of the Turks, and dates back to ancient times. Tarhana is a dough, made with yeast, flour and vegetables – it should be prepared well in advance. Variations of tarhana soup contain cracked or dehusked wheat and can be eaten at any time of day, including breakfast.

FOR THE TARHANA
500g/1lb onions, chopped
500g/1lb peppers, deseeded and chopped
500g/1lb tomatoes, peeled and sliced
a few mint leaves
3tbsp/4 vegetable oil
450ml/³⁄₄ pint suzme yoghurt (p.171)
¹⁄₄tsp fresh yeast
1kg/2lb strong plain flour
1–2tsp salt

Put the vegetables, mint leaves and oil in a heavy-bottomed pan. Cover, and cook on a very low heat for 1–1½ hours until the onions and peppers are tender.

Allow the cooked vegetables to cool until they are just warm, then combine with the remaining ingredients in a mixing bowl, and knead thoroughly. Cover with foil and let the dough rest in a cool place for 10–15 days. Every two days, to prevent the dough from drying out, dip your hands in milk and knead it thoroughly. When the time is up, spread a clean cloth and sprinkle it with flour. Break the dough into lumps and lay them on the cloth. Over the next few days, keep turning the dough to dry it. Finally, when the dough feels only slightly damp, press and roll each lump in the palms of your hands. Put them through a coarse sieve, spread the crumbs once again on a cloth and dry in the sun, or in another warm place. Tarhana is traditionally stored in cotton bags in a cool place. It will keep for up to a year.

NOTE: Tarhana can be made with raw vegetables as well. Mince them, then mix with the other ingredients and pound until you have a stiff purée.

TO SERVE 4
FOR THE SOUP
50g/2oz tarhana
100ml/3¹⁄₂fl oz water
1L/1³⁄₄ pints meat stock (p.33)
50g/2oz clotted cream or kaşar cheese (p.173)
salt as necessary
ACCOMPANIMENT
whole red peppers grilled on embers

Soak the tarhana in the water for 3–4 hours. Heat the stock and when it is warm add the wet tarhana. Let it come to the boil, stirring frequently, then cover, reduce the heat to very low and simmer for 10 minutes. Season to taste.

Pour the hot soup into a tureen. Crumble the clotted cream or grate the kaşar cheese on top of it. Serve with the red peppers.

◊ YOĞURT ÇORBASI ◊

HOT YOGHURT SOUP

Hot yoghurt soup is very popular in Turkey, particularly during the winter. It is usually made with rice in Istanbul cuisine and with pounded cereals in Anatolian cuisine. Both in Istanbul and in Anatolia classic menus for festive meals always start with yoghurt soup.

TO SERVE 4
FOR THE MEAT STOCK
500g/1lb neck, breast, leg meat on bone or 1kg/2lb bones
2.5L/4½ pints water
1 small onion, chopped
1 carrot, chopped
1 stick celery, sliced
1 leek, sliced
a few sprigs parsley
1tbsp rice, washed
3 cloves
4 black peppercorns
2.5cm/1 inch stick cinnamon
1tsp salt
FOR THE SOUP
1L/2 pints stock (above)
25g/1oz dried chickpeas
100g/3½oz rice, picked over and washed
500ml/¾ pint thick yoghurt
2 egg yolks
25g/1oz plain flour
FOR THE DRESSING
50g/2oz butter
1tbsp chopped mint

To prepare the meat stock, place the meat or bones in a pan with the water and bring to the boil. Remove any scum from the top.

Add the remaining ingredients, except the salt. Cover the pan, and when it comes to the boil, reduce the heat and simmer for 2 hours. Add the salt and after 5 minutes remove from the heat and strain the stock. If there is less than 1L/2 pints, top up with water.

To prepare the soup, soak the chickpeas in water for 7–8 hours beforehand. Strain, then put them in a pan with plenty of water and boil on medium heat until cooked.

Put about 1L/2 pints of the meat stock in a pan. Add the rice. Cover and bring to the boil, then continue cooking over a low heat for approximately 15–20 minutes until tender. Strain, saving the liquid. If the amount of liquid has reduced, top it up to 1L/2 pints.

Put a little yoghurt with the egg yolks and flour into a pan and mix well to the consistency of paste. Stir in the rest of the yoghurt, then gradually stir in the rice liquid. Add the strained rice and chickpeas. Heat, and once it comes to the boil cook for 5 minutes, stirring continuously and steadily. Add salt as necessary, stir once more and remove from the heat immediately. (If allowed to boil longer with salt, the yoghurt might separate.)

Pour the soup into a tureen. To make the dressing, heat the butter in a small pan, add the mint, give it a stir and remove at once from the heat. Pour gently over the surface of the soup and serve hot.

NOTE: Yoghurt soup can be prepared and cooked with dehusked wheat instead of rice in exactly the same manner. Soak the wheat with the chickpeas for 7–8 hours beforehand and cook them together.

◊ KURU BAMYA ÇORBASI ◊

DRIED OKRA SOUP

Tiny dried okra, strung like beads, can be seen in many provisions shops in Anatolia. They are used primarily to make this soup. Dried okra soup is particularly popular as a sour-tasting "interval" course in classic menus in Central Anatolia, especially in Konya. A typical Konya wedding menu consists of toyga (yoghurt soup); etli pilav (rice with meat); ırmik helvası (semolina pudding); then okra soup; followed by pilaf and zerde (a sweet rice dish with saffron) and hoşaf (dried fruit compote). The okra soup, restores the appetite for the dishes that follow the dessert!

TO SERVE 4
50g/2oz mutton
50g/2oz sheep's tail or other fat
150g/5oz onions, finely chopped
2tbsp tomato purée
1L/1¾ pints meat stock (p.33)
25g/1oz dried okra
500ml/1 pint water
4tbsp/60ml lemon juice or verjuice (p.173)

salt as necessary
ACCOMPANIMENT
rice pilaf

Slice the meat and fat thinly. Put it in a pan, cover and heat gently. Stir occasionally and when it begins to sizzle, add the onion. Stir for 5 minutes until pale golden. Add the tomato purée and stir a couple of times. Add the stock, and cook for approximately 30 minutes until really tender.

While the meat is cooking, place the okra between two layers of cloth, and rub thoroughly to remove any hairs. Wash well, place in a pan, still on their strings, add the water and 2tbsp lemon juice, cover and boil for 15–20 minutes until half done. (The lemon juice ensures they retain their shape.)

Remove the okra from their strings and add them with the remaining lemon juice or verjuice to the soup. Cover the pan, bring to the boil, reduce to low heat and cook for approximately 20–25 minutes until the okra are tender. Check the seasoning and serve hot.

◊ IŞKEMBE ÇORBASI ◊

TRIPE SOUP

In Turkey tripe soup is usually drunk late in the evening. In large towns there are tripe restaurants – işkembeci – which remain open all night. People who have been out drinking make a final call at the tripe house before returning home.

During the Kurban Bayramı, the religious feast of sacrifice tripe soup is made without fail in every home where the ritual of sacrifice has been observed.

TO SERVE 4
200g/7oz tripe
1L/1¾ pints water
25g/1oz fat
25g/1oz flour
salt
1 egg yolk
1tbsp lemon juice

25g/1oz butter
½tsp red pepper
FOR THE SEASONING
6 cloves garlic
100ml/3½fl oz vinegar
FOR THE GARNISH
3 slices bread

Put the tripe in a pan with the water. Bring to the boil uncovered, then skim off the froth. Cover with the lid and boil for approximately 20 minutes until tender. Add salt and remove from the heat after 5 minutes. Drain the tripe and reserve the cooking liquor. Top up if necessary to 750ml/1¼ pints. Slice the tripe finely.

Melt the fat in a pan and stir in the flour to make a roux. Gradually stir in the cold tripe liquid. Simmer for 5 minutes on very low heat, add the tripe and simmer for a further 5 minutes. Meanwhile, prepare the seasoning: crush the garlic with ¼tsp salt and mix with the vinegar. Prepare the garnish: cut the bread into tiny squares, toast under the grill or fry in butter. Keep hot.

Now beat the egg yolk with the lemon juice. Stir into it a little of the soup liquid, then return to the pan, stirring briskly with a whisk. Season with salt. Allow to boil, then remove from the heat.

Pour the boiling hot soup into a tureen. Melt the butter in a frying pan, add the red pepper, remove from the heat in under a minute, and pour thinly over the surface of the soup. Serve with the garlic vinegar seasoning and croûtons.

◊ TUTMAÇ ÇORBASI ◊
N O O D L E   S O U P

The word "tutmaç" is derived from the expression "Tutma aç", meaning "do not keep us hungry!" Tutmaç was served at a feast in honour of the great Selçuk emperor Tuğrul Bey when he captured the town of Neyshapur, now in northeastern Iran, in 1043. On tasting it the emperor remarked: "The tutmaç is nice but it lacks garlic."

TO SERVE 6
FOR THE PASTA
1 egg
2tbsp water
¼tsp salt
125g/4oz strong plain flour
vegetable oil for deep frying
FOR THE SOUP
250g/8oz mutton shoulder meat, diced
500g/1lb thick-set yoghurt
1 egg
25g/1oz plain flour
3 cloves garlic (optional)
salt as necessary
FOR THE CRACKLINGS
75g/3oz plain flour
1 egg
¼tsp salt
vegetable oil for frying
FOR THE DRESSING
25g/1oz butter
½tsp red pepper

Put the pasta ingredients in a bowl and knead for 10 minutes. Divide the dough into two lumps, cover, and let rest for 20 minutes. Roll out the dough with a long thin rolling pin to a thickness of 3mm/⅛ inch, and cut into 1.25cm/½ inch squares. Dry on a sheet of waxed paper for 20–30 minutes. Deep-fry the pasta squares in oil, and lay out on absorbent paper.

Bring 750ml/1¼ pints water to the boil, add the meat and return to the boil. Skim off the froth and simmer, with the lid on, for approximately 1 hour until tender. Add salt, and remove from the heat after 5 minutes. Top up the liquid if it has diminished.

In another saucepan bring 1L/1¾ pints of water to the boil with 1tbsp each of salt and oil. Add the fried tutmaç pastas, cover and simmer for 15–20 minutes.

For the "cracklings", knead the flour in a bowl with the egg and salt. On a pastry board roll the dough into a long thin stick and slice it finely to resemble lentils. Fry these in oil and lay them out on waxed paper.

In a bowl beat together the yoghurt, egg and flour. Crush the garlic with a little salt and stir into the yoghurt with a little meat stock. Return to the meat.

Strain the tutmaç pastas, and add them to the yoghurt and meat over a low heat, stirring slowly. Bring to the boil, stirring continuously in the same direction. Add salt if necessary and remove from the heat.

Pour the soup into a tureen. For the dressing, heat the butter in a frying pan. Add the red pepper, remove from the heat in under a minute, and pour thinly on the surface of the soup. Sprinkle on some "cracklings", and serve the remainder in a separate dish.

NOTE: Aspur (safflower) can be used instead of red pepper. Do not heat it with the butter, but sprinkle it over the soup after the butter has been poured on.

◊ ARABACI ÇORBASI ◊

ARABACI CHICKEN SOUP

Arabacı is a winter dish from Konya in central Anatolia. During the long winter nights, families and neighbours entertain each other regularly, and on some of those occasions arabacı soup and pişmaniye (a particular kind of helva prepared by the male guests) are served. These gatherings are known as arabacı and pişmaniye evenings.

Everyone helps themselves from a tureen placed in the middle of the table, taking first a small dumpling in the spoon and then some soup, so that the two are consumed together. If anyone drops a dumpling into the soup, then it is that person's turn to invite the guests the following week!

Place the chicken in a pan with 2L/3½ pints cold water. Bring to the boil and skim off the scum. Reduce to low heat and simmer for 1 hour, then add the vegetables, parsley and rice. Cook for a further 1–1½ hours. Add the salt, and after 5 minutes remove from the heat. Strain. If the stock has reduced, top up with hot water. Remove the meat from the bones and cut into small pieces.

To prepare the dumplings, put 1L/ 1¾ pints of the stock in a pan, add the salt and heat until warm. Then take 2 cups of the stock and mix well with the flour. Bring the rest of the stock to the boil, and pour in the flour and stock mixture, stirring briskly. Continue stirring until the mixture thickens, then remove from the heat. Dampen a shallow tray with cold water, pour the batter on to it and leave to set.

To finish the soup, melt the butter, stir in the flour and cook for 3–4 minutes over low heat, stirring all the time, until the flour turns golden. Stir in the tomato purée, add the red pepper and remove from the heat. Add the remaining cold chicken stock, stir well and bring to the boil, stirring constantly. Add the chicken meat, cover and simmer gently for 10 minutes.

Once the batter has set, cut it into diamond-shaped dumplings (like baklava), remove some from the middle of the tray to accommodate the soup tureen, pour the boiling soup into the tureen and serve very hot with a jug of lemon juice.

TO SERVE 6
500g/1lb chicken
1 onion, chopped
1 carrot, chopped
2 sticks celery, chopped
1 leek, sliced
a few sprigs parsley
1tbsp rice
½tbsp salt
50g/2oz butter
50g/2oz plain flour
25g/1oz tomato purée
1tsp red pepper
FOR THE DUMPLINGS
1L/1¾ pints chicken stock
½tsp salt or to taste
100g/3½oz strong plain flour
ACCOMPANIMENT
lemon juice

◊ MEZELER ◊
APPETIZERS

"And in the end thy loved one to thee shall become thy food and water, submissive and obedient and beautiful as well; thy meze and wine too."

MEVLANA'S "MESNEVI" (POEMS)
AND COMMENTARY (1207–73)

On practically every kind of Turkish menu will be offered mezes – a range of hot or cold appetizers. Cold mezes include salads, various kinds of pickles, cheeses, pastırma (dried pressed meat cured with garlic and other spices), savoury sausages, fish roe, caviare, and vegetables cooked in olive oil. Popular hot mezes are pastırma cooked wrapped in paper, eggs with savoury sausages, arnavut ciğeri (liver fried and then cooked in the oven, see p.77), böreks (stuffed savoury pastries), and pilafs.

◊ MIDYE DOLMASI ◊
STUFFED MUSSELS

Stuffed mussels are very popular indeed, particularly in Istanbul and Izmir, and in the latter region it is a favourite home-made dish. By April people start asking each other whether they have had stuffed mussels yet, and shortly after that you find street vendors with baskets full of them at practically every corner.

TO SERVE 3–4
30 large mussels
1 quantity stuffing made with olive oil (p.103)
500ml/17fl oz water
1tsp salt

Prepare the stuffing. Soak the mussels in a bucket of water for 30 minutes. Scrape the shells thoroughly with a knife and wash clean under plenty of running water. Prise the shells open with a knife from the straight side to make butterflies. Cut off the beards and clean.

Put the water and salt in a pan. Rest a colander or steamer above the water.

Stuff the uncooked mussels with the prepared stuffing and close the shells; place them in the colander. To discourage them from opening cover them with a lid or plate and weight down with a clean stone. Steam for 20–30 minutes. Serve cold.

◊ HUMUS ◊
HUMUS

TO SERVE 6
150g/5oz chickpeas
100ml/3½fl oz tahina
3 cloves garlic, crushed
4tbsp lemon juice
4tbsp olive oil
1tsp ground cumin
½tsp red pepper
½tsp salt
3–4 sprigs of parsley
¼tsp coarsely ground red pepper or haspir (p.173)

Soak the chickpeas for 7–8 hours, drain, rinse, then put them in a pan with 1.5L/

2½ pints of fresh water and boil with the lid on, on medium heat for about 2½–3 hours until the chickpeas begin to break up. (If you need to top up, use hot water as the chickpeas will harden otherwise.)

Skim off the chickpea skins while still boiling, then strain the peas and pound them in a mortar. You should have about 250g/8oz chickpea purée. Add the tahina, garlic, lemon juice, half the olive oil, the spices and salt and stir well.

Transfer the humus to a serving dish, pour over it the remaining olive oil and garnish with parsley and coarse red pepper or haspir. Serve cold.

◊ KISIR ◊
BULGUR SALAD

In Turkey ladies have one day a month set aside to receive guests. On those days or on special occasions when a guest arrives, kısır is offered before tea is served.

TO SERVE 4
150g/5oz finely ground bulgur (p.173)
150ml/¼ pint boiling water
100g/3½oz onions, finely chopped
400g/14oz tomatoes, peeled, deseeded and chopped
50g/2oz peppers, deseeded and chopped
25g/1oz parsley, finely chopped
3tbsp olive oil
½tsp red pepper; salt
1tbsp pomegranate syrup (p.173) or 2tbsp lemon juice

ACCOMPANIMENTS
boiled vine leaves or red cabbage leaves
pickles, sliced tomatoes

Put the bulgur in a bowl and stir in the water a few spoonfuls at a time. Cover with a lid, and let it rest for 15 minutes at room temperature.

Add the onion to the bulgur, and combine thoroughly. Then stir in the other ingredients, seasoning to taste.

Line a serving dish with vine leaves and serve the kısır on them or serve it spooned into red cabbage leaves, making one helping per leaf, together with sliced tomatoes and pickles.

◊ ÇERKEZ TAVUĞU ◊
CIRCASSIAN CHICKEN

TO SERVE 4–6
1kg/2lb chicken pieces
1 onion, chopped
1 carrot, chopped
1 stick celery, sliced
1 leek, sliced
a few sprigs parsley
1tbsp rice, washed
3 cloves
1tsp salt
50g/2oz butter
50g/2oz onions, finely chopped
FOR THE WALNUT SAUCE
125g/4oz shelled walnuts
50g/2oz breadcrumbs
1 clove garlic
2tsp red pepper
200ml/7fl oz chicken stock
FOR THE DRESSING
3–4tbsp/45–60ml walnut oil
¼tsp red pepper

To poach the chicken, bring 1L/1¾ pints of water to the boil and add the meat, vegetables, parsley, rice and cloves. Simmer on a low heat until the chicken is just cooked (30–40 minutes) – it should not be too soft. Add the salt, and after 5 minutes remove from the heat. Strain the stock, and shred the chicken.

Melt the butter in another pan. Fry the onion, stirring frequently until lightly coloured. Add the shredded chicken and 200ml/7fl oz of hot stock, and heat gently, uncovered, for approximately 10 minutes until the liquid has evaporated. Transfer the chicken and onion to a serving dish.

With a pestle and mortar pound together the ingredients for the walnut sauce, or blend in a food processor. Pour the sauce over the chicken, sprinkle over the oil and red pepper and serve cold.

◊ MUHAMMARA ◊
SPICED WALNUT PASTE

TO SERVE 6
75g/3oz shelled walnuts
25g/1oz tomato purée
25g/1oz breadcrumbs
2tbsp olive oil
1tbsp pomegranate syrup (p.173) or lemon juice
1tsp coarsely ground red pepper
1tsp ground cumin
1tsp sugar

Pound the walnuts to a paste in a mortar, then mix in all the other ingredients. Alternatively, put everything in a liquidizer or food processor and blend to a paste. Serve at room temperature.

◊ FAVA ◊

PURÉED BROAD BEANS

TO SERVE 6
250g/8oz dried broad beans
150g/5oz onions, quartered
3tbsp/45ml olive oil
1L/1¾ pints water
1tsp caster sugar
1tsp salt
2tbsp finely chopped dill
FOR THE DRESSING
2tbsp/30ml olive oil
2tbsp/30ml lemon juice
FOR THE GARNISH
5–6 sprigs of dill
lemon slices

Wash the dried beans, soak in water for 8 hours, then strain and wash again. Put the beans into a pan with the onions, olive oil, water, sugar and salt. Cover and cook on a low heat for 40 minutes or until the beans break up. While still hot strain and purée through a coarse sieve or in a food processor – the mixture should have the consistency of thick yoghurt.

Put the purée in a pan over gentle heat, add the dill, and let it bubble for 1 minute while stirring. Transfer the purée to a serving dish, and leave to cool for 1–2 hours. Beat together the olive oil and lemon juice and pour over the purée. Garnish with dill sprigs and lemon slices.

NOTE: Another way of serving fava is to cook the purée for 5 minutes, then pour it into a flat dish about 22cm/8 inches in diameter. Once cold cut into diamond shapes. Dress with oil and lemon juice and garnish.

◊ ÇÖKELEKLI BIBER KAVURMASI ◊

CHEESE WITH GREEN PEPPERS

This dish of hot curd cheese and green peppers is a speciality of Edirne, the principal city of Thrace (the European part of Turkey). Sunflowers are cultivated extensively in this region, so the oil is widely used in the local cooking. Çökelek is a kind of curd cheese made by adding salt to yoghurt and boiling it. The action of the salt and the heat breaks down the milk proteins to produce curds – çökelek.

TO SERVE 4
100g/3½oz green peppers, deseeded and chopped
3tbsp/45ml sunflower oil
250g/8oz çökelek – curd cheese
FOR THE GARNISH
½tsp coarsely ground red pepper

Fry the peppers in the oil on medium heat for 7–8 minutes, stirring continuously. Add the curd cheese, reduce the heat, and fry for 1–2 minutes while stirring until the cheese and peppers are thoroughly mixed. Remove the pan from the heat.

Transfer the mixture to a serving dish – a copper dish with a notched rim is traditional. Sprinkle red pepper over it and serve warm – though it can be eaten cold as well.

◊ ÇİNGENE PİLAVI ◊

 GIPSY PILAF

This pilaf comes from Aydın, on the Aegean, where it is invariably served on market days. When the housewife returns home, tired out from shopping in the market, she prepares gipsy pilaf as it is easy to make and also uses up any bruised vegetables.

The dish is called Gispy Pilaf because gipsies tend to eat a lot of raw foods as they are constantly travelling

TO SERVE 6
250g/8oz white cheese or çökelek
salt as necessary
100g/3½oz onions, finely chopped
150g/4oz tomatoes, peeled and coarsely chopped
50g/2oz green pointed peppers, finely sliced
2tbsp olive oil
2tbsp chopped parsley

Grate the cheese into a bowl. Add a little salt to the onions, mix and crush to release the juice. Stir the onions into the cheese with the tomatoes, peppers and olive oil.

Place on a serving dish. Garnish with parsley and serve at room temperature.

◊ BATIRIK ◊

BULGUR PATTIES

Batırık is another southern dish based on bulgur paste and tomatoes, but it includes nuts. Like kısır it is offered before tea is served, or, indeed, at any time of the day. It can be made with sesame seeds instead of pistachio nuts or walnuts. A liquid version can be made by adding 500ml/ 1 pint water to the ingredients listed below, and eaten with a spoon.

TO SERVE 6
150g/5oz finely ground bulgur
300g/10oz tomatoes, peeled, deseeded and pulped
1tsp tomato purée
100g/3½oz onions, finely sliced
25g/1oz green peppers, shredded
100g/3½oz walnuts or pistachio nuts
1tsp chilli flakes
salt as necessary
1tbsp chopped parsley
1tbsp chopped basil or majoram

ACCOMPANIMENTS
sliced tomatoes
green peppers

Spread the bulgur on a tray. Add the tomatoes and tomato purée, and mix very thoroughly by hand. Then add the onion and pepper and knead until combined. Either pound thoroughly or process the walnuts or pistachios. Add them to the mixture and knead until the bulgur and other ingredients are thoroughly mixed and stick together. Add the chilli flakes and salt as required with the parsley and basil and knead until properly mixed. In the palms of the hands form into small flattish balls.

Arrange on a serving dish with slices of tomatoes and green peppers. Serve immediately without letting them stand.

◊ MIRTOĞA ◊

Mirtoğa is a breakfast favourite in eastern Anatolia, a speciality of Van, and a simple dish one can never tire of, particularly when it is served with the delicious and distinctive local herb cheese (p.28), the renowned honey from Kars and tea prepared in a samovar.

Throughout Anatolia there are a number of foods which are traditionally regarded as a suitable first meal for a mother following the birth of her child. Mirtoğa is one of the most highly recommended.

TO SERVE 3–4
2 eggs
¼tsp salt
125g/4oz butter
100g/3½oz plain flour

ACCOMPANIMENT

honey

In a bowl beat the eggs and salt thoroughly with a fork.

In a small frying pan melt the butter on medium heat, add the flour and fry, stirring with a wooden spoon for 5–7 minutes until the flour colours. Pour on the eggs, stirring quickly. Keep shaking the frying pan until the bottom of the omelette is pinkish, then turn it over with a skimmer and cook the other side. Serve the mirtoğa hot with honey drizzled over it.

◊ YUMURTALAR ◊
E G G   D I S H E S

*I*n Turkey many people rear chickens in their own backyards, and as a consqeuence, eggs are an important part of the diet. Their value in Turkish cuisine is symbolic as well as nutritional. In southeastern Anatolia in particular eggs play a central part in popular customs at ceremonies and festivities. In Siirt the first week in May is celebrated as the Egg Festival. On the first day of the festival hard-boiled eggs are prepared in every home and taken on picnics out in the country where entertainments are organized. Youngsters engage in egg-shelling competitions and young girls and men spend the holiday getting to know one another: tradition has it that this is the time for betrothals.

When a girl gets engaged, her prospective mother-in-law sends her 250 raw and 250 cooked eggs as a gift. The girl makes a present of the cooked eggs to her fiancé, and uses the raw ones at home. Once married, she is under an obligation to present her mother-in-law with a gift of eggs on each Egg Festival, until her death.

In Şanlı Urfa the letters written by a young man doing his military service are kept until he completes it and returns home. Then the letters are burnt and an egg is fried over the flames and served to him to celebrate the occasion.

Another Anatolian festival, Hıdırellez, celebrates the arrival of spring on 6 May, the 40th day after the spring equinox. People take picnics into the country and resolve "to shed the past year's worries and troubles like the shell of an egg" – so saying, they shell boiled eggs and eat them.

◊ SUCUKLU YUMURTA ◊
E G G   W I T H   S P I C Y   S A U S A G E S

This is a favourite dish for breakfast and for Iftar – the meal that breaks the fast of Ramadan.

TO SERVE 3
60g/2½oz butter
100g/3½oz spicy sausages, finely sliced
3tbsp/45ml water
6 eggs
salt as necessary
shallow 30cm/12 inch pan

Melt the butter in the pan on medium heat. Add the sausages and fry for 2 minutes, turning them over frequently. Add the water, and cover with a lid. When it starts to boil, clear six places between the pieces of sausage, crack the eggs in the spaces, sprinkle a little salt on each, replace the lid, and cook on very low heat for 3–4 minutes. Serve while hot.

NOTE: Eggs with pastırma (p.173) may be cooked in the same way.

◊ KIYMALI YUMURTA ◊

MINCED MEAT AND EGGS

TO SERVE 3
25g/1oz butter
200g/7oz onions, sliced
150g/5oz minced meat
50g/2oz green peppers, finely chopped
½tsp salt, or as necessary
100g/3½oz tomatoes, peeled and diced
1tbsp chopped parsley
100ml/3½fl oz water
6 eggs
shallow 30cm/12 inch pan

Heat the butter in the pan and fry the onions for 3–4 minutes until golden. Add the minced meat and peppers. Fry for 8–10 minutes until the meat absorbs its own juice; add salt, and continue to cook, turning over the contents of the pan for 2 minutes. Add the tomatoes, parsley and water. Cover with a lid, bring to the boil, then reduce to very low heat and cook gently for 10 minutes. With a spoon make six hollows in the mixture and crack an egg into each one. Sprinkle a little salt on each egg, cover with a lid and cook for 3–4 minutes on very low heat. Serve immediately while hot.

◊ ÇILBIR ◊

POACHED EGG WITH YOGHURT

TO SERVE 2–3
1 quantity yoghurt and garlic sauce (p.172)
6 eggs
FOR POACHING
1L/1¾ pints water
1tbsp salt
1tbsp vinegar
FOR THE GARNISH
50g/2oz butter
6 sage leaves
¼tsp red pepper

Prepare the yoghurt and garlic sauce and pour into a serving dish.

Bring the water to the boil with the salt and vinegar, pop the eggs into it, cover with a lid, lower the heat, and poach the eggs for 2–3 minutes until the whites stiffen while the yolks remain soft. Remove the eggs with a perforated ladle and place them on the yoghurt sauce.

In a frying pan heat the butter with the sage leaves, add the pepper, remove from the heat in under a minute and pour over the eggs. Serve hot.

◊

FISH AND SEAFOOD

◊

◊ BALIKLAR ◊

FISH DISHES

Turkish cooking is rich in fish and seafood dishes, not surprising since the country is surrounded on three sides by sea. The Black Sea coast is particularly renowned for the variety of its fish cookery, from plain baked, grilled and fried fish of superb quality, to imaginative stews and pilafs.

In the Muslim faith fish and bread symbolize fertility. In the Koran it is stated that the Lord caused a table to descend from heaven for Jesus Christ. According to Anatolian folklore, there were two fishes and five loaves of bread on the table, and after 5,000 men, women and children had eaten their fill, there were still 12 large baskets of fish and bread left over. For this reason fish and bread are held in particularly high esteem in Anatolia.

◊ KAĞITTA LEVREK ◊

SEA BASS EN PAPILLOTTE

TO SERVE 4
1kg/2lb bass, filleted (4 pieces)
200g/7oz onions, finely chopped
100g/3½oz butter
1kg/2lb tomatoes, skinned and deseeded
½tsp salt
1.25cm/½ inch stick of cinnamon
3 cloves
1 bay leaf
4 "teardrops" mastic (p.173)
¼tsp salt

Fry the onions in the butter for 3 minutes, add the tomatoes, salt, spices and bayleaf. Cover the pan and bring to the boil, then lower the heat and cook for 10 minutes. Press the sauce through a sieve.

Put each fillet of fish on a piece of foil. Beat the mastic with ¼tsp salt and sprinkle on the fish. Pour a quarter of the sauce over each fillet, wrap up the parcels and set them on a baking tray. Brush with water and bake in a preheated oven at 200°C/400°F/gas mark 6, and cook for about 10 minutes. Serve the papillottes at once, to be opened at the table.

◊ BALIK IZGARA ◊

GRILLED FISH

Çipura is a very common fish to be found along the Aegean coast and it is much liked in Izmir. It is best eaten grilled over charcoal. It can also be dipped in flour and fried. Small mackerel, red mullet or snapper can be prepared in the same way, as can steaks of larger fish.

TO SERVE 4
4 çipura or other small fish
300g/10oz onions
½tsp salt
FOR THE MARINADE
onion juice (see below)
2tbsp olive oil
2tbsp lemon juice
¼tsp ground black pepper
1tsp salt
10 bay leaves
FOR BASTING
2tbsp olive oil
2tbsp lemon juice
FOR THE SEASONING SAUCE
1 egg yolk
2tbsp lemon juice
2tbsp olive oil
4 "teardrops" of mastic (p.173)
¼tsp salt
FOR THE GARNISH
4 sprigs parsley
1tbsp onion juice (see below)
lemon slices

Onion juice is used for all kinds of fish and meat dishes in Turkey. To prepare it, grate the onions, crush with the salt, and leave to stand for 2 minutes. Then put the onions in a muslin cloth, and squeeze to extract the juice: there should be about 100ml/3½fl oz. Reserve 1tbsp juice and mix the rest with the ingredients for the marinade.

Clean and wash the fish, leaving the heads on. Let them drain for 5 minutes, then brush inside and out with the marinade and leave to stand for 2 hours in a cold pantry or in the fridge.

Just before cooking beat the lemon juice with the olive oil. Have a small brush ready for basting. Beat together all the ingredients for the seasoning sauce. Leave it to stand in a cool place. Mix the parsley with the reserved onion juice for the garnish.

Brush the grill with the basting liquid and place the fish on it. Place the grill 10cm/4 inches above the glowing coals and cook for 10–20 minutes – depending on the size of the fish – turning them as they cook and brushing on more basting liquor when they become dry.

Place the grilled fish on a serving dish. Put the chopped parsley in their mouths and garnish with lemon slices. Pour over the seasoning sauce, and serve hot, with a tomato salad.

◊ USKUMRU DOLMASI ◊

STUFFED MACKEREL

Mackerel is very popular in Turkey. You will find it grilled, fried, sautéed, and cooked with vegetables. This recipe for stuffed mackerel is quite unusual. The fish must be very fresh because the skin must be left intact although the flesh and bones are removed. It is then stuffed with the cooked fish and deep-fried.

TO SERVE 4
4 mackerel (total weight about 1kg/2lb), cleaned through the gills and heads left on (see below)
3–4tbsp/45–60ml olive oil
400g/14oz onions, finely chopped
50g/2oz pine nuts
25g/1oz currants
1tsp ground cinnamon
1tsp ground cloves
1tsp ground allspice
1tsp ground black pepper
salt as necessary
4tbsp/60ml chopped parsley
4tbsp/60ml dill
25g/1oz plain flour
olive or vegetable oil for deep-frying
FOR THE GARNISH
½tsp ground cinnamon
½tsp ground cloves
½tsp allspice

To prepare the fish, make a cut, as if to sever the head from the body, just above the gills, but leave the head attached at the backbone. Remove the gills and insert your finger to remove the innards. Wash the fish thoroughly, inside and out. Pound gently with a mallet to soften the flesh and break the backbone in several places. Snip the backbone behind the head so that the head remains attached only by skin.

Force the flesh and bones upwards from the tail by pressing and squeezing. Make sure you do not puncture the skin. Discard the bones and finely chop or mince the flesh.

Pour the olive oil into a frying pan. Add the onions and pine nuts, fry for about 5 minutes until the onions turn golden, then add the fish. Fry for 4–5 minutes until the fish turns white. Stir in the currants and spices, season with salt and remove from the heat. Mix in the parsley and dill and leave to cool.

Fill the fish skins with the cooled stuffing. Roll them in flour and fry in hot oil for 5 minutes. Remove and drain on greaseproof paper.

Place the fish on a heated serving dish, combine the spices for the garnish, sprinkle them over and serve.

◊ PALAMUT PAPAZ YAHNISI ◊

TUNA OR BONITO STEW

Striped tuna or bonito are most popular in Turkey for this dish, but substitute grey mullet, mackerel or gurnard if you prefer. The fish stock can be used for any fish dish or soup and forms the basis of this flavoursome stew, redolent of garlic and spices.

TO SERVE 3–4
FOR THE FISH STOCK
750g/1½lb white fish or 1.25kg/3lb fish trimmings
25g/1oz butter
150g/5oz onions, chopped
1 carrot, chopped
1 leek, sliced
1 stick celery, sliced
3 cloves garlic, chopped
3 sprigs parsley, chopped
2 bay leaves
½tsp dried thyme
1tsp salt
2L/3½ pints water
FOR THE STEW
500g/1lb striped tuna, filleted
½tsp salt
4tbsp/60ml olive oil
300g/10oz onions, finely sliced
100g/3½oz carrots, finely sliced
10 cloves of garlic (or more), halved
1tbsp tomato purée
½tsp cinnamon
½tsp red pepper
300ml/½ pint fish stock
2tbsp lemon juice or vinegar
3 sprigs parsley, chopped

To prepare the fish stock, heat the butter in a large pan and brown the vegetables for 3 minutes. Add the fish or fish trimmings with the remaining ingredients and pour on the water. Bring to the boil, skim off the froth and cover the pan. Let it simmer for 30 minutes on a low heat, then strain. If the stock is reduced to under 1L/1¾ pints, top it up with hot water.

For the stew, rinse the fish in cold running water, then rub with salt and lay them to drain.

Heat the oil and onions for 10 minutes, stirring from time to time. Add the carrots and garlic and fry for another 5 minutes. Add the tomato purée and stir for 1 minute.

Cover the bottom of a large pan with half the mixture. Place the fish fillets on it in a row and spread over them the remainder of the onion mixture.

Stir the cinnamon, red pepper and ½tsp of salt into the hot fish stock and pour over the fish. Add the lemon juice or vinegar, cover the pan and cook for 25–30 minutes over medium heat until the fish is tender. Let it cool, garnish with parsley and serve cold straight from the pan.

◊ HAMSI PILAVI ◊

ANCHOVY PILAF

Anchovies are a great favourite along the Black Sea coast and different methods of cooking them are hotly debated; in fact the people of the region are often teased that they would even make jam out of anchovies! This recipe, which comes from Trabzon, combines anchovies with rice in an unusual pie-like pilaf. You can reduce the amount of spices to suit your taste and use small fresh sardines instead of the anchovies.

TO SERVE 4–6
1kg/2lb anchovies or sardines
2tbsp olive oil
FOR THE PILAF
250g/8oz rice
salt
250g/8oz onions, finely sliced
3tbsp/45ml water
100ml/3½fl oz olive oil
50g/2oz raisins
50g/2oz pine nuts
500ml/17fl oz boiling water
1tbsp caster sugar
½tsp ground black pepper
½tsp ground cinnamon
½tsp dried thyme
1tbsp chopped mint
FOR THE GARNISH
100g/3½oz butter

Remove the heads and backbones from the fish and open them flat. Rinse them, sprinkle them with a little salt, and drain in a colander.

Put the rice in a pan, cover with warm water with 1tbsp of salt and leave until it gets cool, then rinse until the water runs clear, and drain.

Put the onions, water and ½tsp salt in a pan on medium heat, stirring from time to time, for about 10 minutes or until the onions absorb their juices. Pour on the oil and fry for 4–5 minutes, then add the rice and fry for 5–6 minutes stirring occasionally, until the rice begins to stick to the bottom of the pan. Stir in the raisins and pine nuts, pour on the boiling water and add the sugar. Cover the pan, boil for 5 minutes on medium heat, then reduce to low heat and simmer gently for about 10 minutes until the rice absorbs the liquid and holes appear in the surface. Remove from the heat, stir in the spices and herbs, cover the pan and let it rest for 10 minutes.

Brush a wide, flat-bottomed casserole with olive oil. Cover the base of it with about half of the anchovies, skin sides down, and arrange a row of anchovies around the sides of the casserole (like the case of a pie). Fill the "case" with the rice and cover the top with the remaining anchovies, skin sides up. Sprinkle with oil.

Heat the oven to 200°C/400°F/gas mark 6, and cook for 30–40 minutes until the anchovies turn golden brown.

Heat the butter in a pan and pour gently all over the surface. Serve the fish in the pan.

◊ LEVREK PILAKISI ◊

SEA BASS STEW

Swordfish, bonito or striped tuna may be used in this garlicky fish and potato stew, instead of bass.

TO SERVE 4
500g/1lb bass, filleted
salt
3–4tbsp/45–60ml olive oil
250g/8oz onions, thinly sliced
300g/10oz celery, sliced
100g/3½oz carrots, sliced
10 cloves of garlic, peeled and left whole
300g/10oz tomatoes, peeled and deseeded
300g/10oz potatoes, peeled and sliced
200ml/7fl oz fish stock (p.50)
½tsp red pepper
1 lemon, sliced, peel and pith removed
FOR THE GARNISH
a handful of chopped parsley
juice of half a lemon

Rinse the fish under cold running water, sprinkle with salt and leave to drain.

Heat the olive oil and fry the onions, celery, carrots and garlic for 3 minutes. Then add the tomatoes, potatoes, fish stock, pepper and a pinch of salt, cover the pan and cook for 10 minutes.

Cover the bottom of a large shallow pan with half the vegetable mixture, place the fish fillets on it and spread over them the remainder of the mixture with its liquid; place the lemon slices on top. Cover the pan and cook for about 30 minutes until the vegetables and fish are tender.

Serve cold sprinkled with chopped parsley, together with the lemon juice.

◊ KALKAN TAVA ◊

FRIED TURBOT

TO SERVE 3–4
1kg/2lb turbot, cleaned
1 quantity fish marinade (p.48)
olive oil or vegetable oil for deep-frying
50g/2oz flour
FOR THE GARNISH
lemon slices
chopped parsley
ACCOMPANIMENT
onion salad (p.117)

Cut the fish into strips 2.5cm/1 inch wide and 10cm/4 inches long. Rinse and drain. Marinate for 2 hours in the fish marinade, then drain.

Heat the oil. Coat the strips of fish in flour, shake off any excess and deep-fry for 6–7 minutes until golden. Remove and drain on absorbent paper.

Put the lemon slices around the edge of a heated serving dish, put the fish in the middle and sprinkle with chopped parsley. Serve with an onion salad and lemon juice.

◊ KEFAL FIRINDA ◊

BAKED GREY MULLET

TO SERVE 4
1kg/2lb grey mullet, cleaned
small bunch of parsley
300ml/½ pint water
400g/14oz onions, sliced
400g/14oz tomatoes, skinned and pulped or 25g/1oz tomato purée
100ml/3½fl oz olive oil
1tsp salt
1tsp red pepper
1tsp ground cinnamon
½tsp ground cloves
2tbsp flour
FOR THE GARNISH
4 "teardrops" mastic (p.173)
½tsp salt
juice of half a lemon

Cut the mullet into steaks or fillets, rinse them and place in a shallow pan.

Boil the parsley, including the stalks, in the water for 5 minutes, then strain and reserve the liquid. Put the onions and tomato pulp or purée in a bowl and stir in the olive oil. Add the salt, spices, flour and parsley liquid and mix thoroughly. Pour the mixture over the fish. Cook in a pre-heated oven at 200°C/400°F/gas mark 6, for 25–30 minutes or until the fish is tender.

Pound the mastic with the salt and lemon juice and sprinkle over the fish when you take it out of the oven. Serve hot or cold.

◊ KIREMITTE LÜFER ◊

SEA PERCH BAKED ON A TILE

Sea perch on a tile is a recipe from the Black Sea coast. This form of cooking, using the long curved roofing tiles of the region, is particularly favoured by construction workers who take the dish to the local baker to have it cooked in his oven.

Nowadays this dish is cooked in restaurants and homes in an earthenware dish.

TO SERVE 2
1 sea perch of about 500g/1lb, cleaned
½tsp salt
½ quantity fish marinade (p.48)
50g/2oz butter, melted
a few cabbage leaves
a handful of chopped parsley
lemon wedges

Rinse the fish under running water, sprinkle with salt, and leave to drain for 5 minutes. Marinate for 1 hour.

Heat the tile or dish in a hot oven for 10 minutes. When it is cool enough to handle brush with half the butter, line it with a cabbage leaf or two and place the fish on it. Brush the remaining butter on the fish, and enclose it completely in cabbage leaves. Bake in a preheated oven at 250°C/500°F/gas mark 10, for 20–25 minutes.

Remove upper cabbage leaf, scoop butter over the fish; garnish with parsley.

◊

MEAT

◊

◊ ETLER ◊

MEAT DISHES

From ancient times to this day meat has been the most important element of Turkish cuisine. Kebabs, boiled meat dishes and stews are mentioned in the earliest Turkish written sources. The 11th-century Classical Turkish Dictionary has a reference to men who "competed against each other in skewering meat". Today the town of Gaziantep in southeastern Anatolia is renowned throughout Turkey for the variety and superb quality of its kebabs.

There are dozens of varieties of kebabs which may be grilled, baked or even stewed. Some are named for the way they are cooked: tandır kebabı in a pit oven or tandır; şiş kebabı on şiş or skewers; others after a place, such as Adana or Sanlı Urfa, depending upon the way the meat is cut and spiced.

Mutton and lamb are the most popular meat; the fat-tailed sheep can be seen all over the Anatolian plain, and the fat is much prized for its succulence and flavour.

Köfte, rissoles or meatballs, made of minced and pounded meat with a wide range of seasonings are another speciality.

In Turkey meat is even used in certain fruit dishes and other desserts, such as tavuk göğsü, a classic pudding made with breast of chicken, and gerdan tatlısı, made with scrag end of neck of lamb.

KEBABS

◊ IZGARA KEBABLARI ◊

GRILLED KEBABS

The best kebabs are made with meat from a male sheep between 18 months and two years old. Meat freshly cut on the day that the animal is slaughtered is ideal.

Before cooking, any gristle must be removed, otherwise the kebabs will be tough. For a tasty minced meat kebab, the meat should not be put through a mincer – this bruises the meat and causes moisture loss; it should be finely chopped with a cleaver.

In Turkey lambs do not have their tails docked and the fat from the tail is widely used in cooking. When making kebabs a slice of tail is threaded on after every two or three cubes of meat to add flavour and make the meat more tender. Fat from another part of the animal may be used instead. For kebabs of minced meat, depending on the kind of meat being used, 30–50 per cent tail fat is mixed in.

Kebabs of meat cubes should be marinated for 10–12 hours before grilling. Kebabs of minced meat must be cooked immediately once the vegetables or other additional ingredients have been kneaded in.

If the kebabs are to be served with any kind of sauce, prepare the sauce before cooking the kebabs. Once the kebabs have been dressed they must be served without delay, otherwise the sauce will make them soft and they will lose their flavour.

For the best flavour kebabs should be cooked over charcoal.

KEBAB MARINADES In Istanbul onion juice is a favourite marinade. Use one quantity of juice as described on p.48 for 500g/1lb meat. Nowadays 1tbsp olive oil is generally added to this quantity of juice. Use for any kebab.

The recipe below comes from Gaziantep and will marinate 500g/1lb meat.

2 cloves garlic
¼tsp salt
2tbsp olive oil
1tsp tomato purée
½tsp red pepper
pinch of black pepper
pinch of ground allspice

pinch of ground cinnamon
pinch of ground cumin
pinch of dried thyme
1tbsp water

Pound the garlic with the salt. Mix with the other ingredients. Rub the mixture on the meat and let it rest for 12 hours.

BASTING LIQUOR A basting liquor will seal in the flavour of the meat and prevent it from scorching over the coals. Make a meat stock according to the instructions on p.33. Let it cool, so that the fat sets on the surface. Remove the fat and melt it over gentle heat. Mix it with an equal amount of the stock and use to coat the grill as well as to baste the meat.

◊ ŞİŞ KEBABI ◊

KEBAB ON SKEWERS

You can use either of the marinades described above for these kebabs.

TO SERVE 2–3
400g/14oz leg of lamb
1 quantity marinade
100g/3½oz sheep's tail or other fat
500g/1lb tomatoes, halved
100g/3½oz green peppers, cut into squares
basting liquid (above)
ACCOMPANIMENT
rice pilaf (p.119)
metal skewers

Remove the sinewy parts of the meat and cut the meat and fat into 3cm/1¼ inch cubes. Rub in the marinade and leave for 12 hours in a glass or china bowl. Thread on skewers with one piece of fat to every three of meat.

Grill both sides of the vegetables and place on a serving dish.

Position the skewers 10cm/4 inches above a charcoal fire and grill for 4–6 minutes, turning them over and basting with a brush as they dry.

Remove the meat from the skewers and place on the serving dish with the grilled vegetables. Serve hot with rice pilaf.

"Where there is wine, kebab and a lyre, cares and concerns are banished from such a place; they entertain no such limitations."

(MEVLANA'S VERSES, 24, 3)

◊ KABURGA DOLMASI ◊

STUFFED BREAST OF KID

TO SERVE 6–8
1 breast of year-old kid, 2.5–3kg/5–6lb
FOR THE STUFFING
300g/10oz rice
1tbsp salt
150g/5oz whole shelled almonds
200g/7oz shoulder of lamb, diced
100g/3¹⁄₂oz butter
1tbsp very finely chopped basil
1tsp ground black pepper
1tsp ground allspice
1tsp salt
25g/1oz tomato purée
ACCOMPANIMENT
ayran (p.168)

Soak the rice in 500ml/1 pint warm salted water. Blanch the almonds.

Sear the lamb in a pan for 5–10 minutes until it absorbs all its juices. Add 500ml/1 pint boiling water and cook for 30–40 minutes until the meat is tender. If the liquid reduces, top up with more boiling water.

Melt half the butter in a pan. Drain and rinse the rice and add to the butter. Brown for 5 minutes, stirring carefully in order not to break up the grains. When the rice begins to stick to the bottom of the pan, add the cooked meat with its liquid. Partly cook the rice by boiling for 3 minutes on high heat, then lower the heat to medium for 3 minutes, then simmer for 5 minutes on very low heat. Remove from the heat, place a cloth between the pan and the lid and let it rest for 10 minutes.

Melt the remaining butter in a small pan. Add the almonds and stir until golden. Mix the basil and almonds into the rice and season with the spices.

58

Cut an opening in the breast between the flesh and bone, and stuff with the partly cooked rice mixture. This must be done very carefully: if the stuffing is too loosely packed it will let in water; if too densely it will burst open. Sew up the slit and brush over with tomato purée.

Grease a large casserole. Place it on the heat and brown the fleshy part of the breast for 4–5 minutes, then turn it over so that the bony part is at the bottom. Pour on 500ml/1 pint boiling water, cover and cook on low heat for 1 hour. Turn over so that the meaty part is at the bottom and cook on extremely low heat for a further 4–5 minutes.

Place the meat on a carving dish, cut and remove the string. Serve hot with ayran.

NOTE: The stuffed breast can be cooked without brushing with tomato purée, but after cooking it should be roasted briefly in the oven to give it a deeper colour.

◊ YUFKALI SAÇ KEBABI ◊

KEBABS IN A POUCH

TO SERVE 4–6
50g/2oz sheep's tail or cooking fat
250g/8oz medium fat leg of lamb
100g/3½oz onions, thinly sliced
50g/2oz red or green peppers, finely chopped
200g/7oz tomatoes, peeled, deseeded and chopped or 25g/1oz tomato purée
1tsp vinegar
½tsp red pepper
¼tsp ground black pepper
¼tsp ground cinnamon
¼tsp ground cumin
salt to taste
¼tsp dried thyme
a few sprigs each dill and parsley, finely chopped
100ml/3½fl oz hot water
FOR THE YUFKA
125g/4oz plain flour
125g/4oz strong plain flour
1tsp salt
500ml/17fl oz water

Dice the tail or fat and meat. Put the tail or fat in a baking tin on the heat, and stir until the tail has yielded its fat, or the fat has melted. Add the meat and brown until it absorbs its juices. Add the onions and peppers, and cook, stirring, until the onions are golden. Add the tomato, cook for a few minutes, then add the other ingredients. Cover the pan and simmer on a very low heat for 1–1½ hours until the meat is tender, adding a little more hot water if necessary.

To make yufka, sieve the flours into a small bowl and add the salt. Add the water gradually to start with, allowing the flour to absorb it. When the flour is wet through, add the rest of the water and whisk. The consistency should be rather like that of pancake batter. Rest for 1–2 minutes.

Heat the saç or frying pan and oil it with a tiny piece of butter. Pour in one ladleful of the batter and shake the pan to spread it all over. When one side has cooked, turn and cook the other side for 1–2 minutes. Repeat until all the yufka are cooked. This amount should make 6–7.

Divide the filling between the yufka, fold over the sides and serve hot.

◊ ÇEBIÇ ◊

SPIT-ROASTED WHOLE KID OR LAMB

Çebiç is a delicious meal served at big parties in Konya. The 11th-century Classical Turkish Dictionary describes çebiç as "a whole lamb kebabed in a pit dug in the earth". The ovens at the Çatalhöyük archaeological site resemble the modern tandır or oven pit, indicating that this style of cooking dates back many thousands of years.

Nowadays guests are invited to come in the morning and spend the whole day at parties given in homes with orchards or vineyards and gardens and a tandır in the grounds. For breakfast there is home-grown and homemade food – bread, butter, cream, cheese, thick-set yoghurt made by the lady of the household from the milk of a sheep or a cow or two kept on the property; honey, jams made from morello cherries, apricots, strawberries, cornelian cherries, or crabapple with grape syrup (pekmez, p.173); peppers, cucumbers, tomatoes, and a variety of fruits picked in the garden. The pride of place at the breakfast table is accorded to the liver of the animal to be used for the çebiç. The liver is cut in very thin slices, the surface is finely slit into squares with a sharp knife, and then it is grilled.

After breakfast the guests are encouraged to go for a long walk. On their return the çebiç is served.

The menu for a çebiç meal includes yoghurt soup; çebiç; bulgur pilaf; su böreği – a light layered pie filled with cheese or minced meat; höşmerim (p.141), or baklava; okra soup; stuffed vine leaves; rice pilaf; and fruit compote. In between courses the guests' palates are refreshed with thick-set yoghurt, pickles, salads, ayran – a yoghurt drink – and fruit juices.

After the meal the guests are invited to take advantage of the shade provided by the orchard or garden to take an hour's nap. Then a neighbour pays a call to invite the whole company to come over to his or her property for a party known as "Rousing the Neighbour". At this party the spread features a dish made with home-grown vegetables such as fresh beans cooked with meat, marrow with eggs or aubergines in olive oil with onions and tomatoes. Naturally the guests are also offered roast meat or savoury pastries.

After the feast, the guests drift back to the house of their hosts, where they are presented with baskets of home-grown produce before finally making their way home.

1 kid or lamb (under a year old)
100g/3½oz shallots, slivered
25g/1oz garlic, slivered
FOR THE MARINADE
200g/7oz thick-set yoghurt
150g/5oz tomato purée
100g/3½oz onions, very finely chopped
25g/1oz garlic, very finely chopped
50g/2oz salt
FOR THE GARNISH
parsley soaked in onion juice (p.48) for 5 minutes
flowers of the season
ACCOMPANIMENT
bulgur pilaf (p.119) cooked in the juices of the çebiç

Traditionally the lamb is slaughtered on the day it is to be roasted. The horns are removed without damaging the head, the carcass is skinned, and the internal organs removed. All this is done carefully and cleanly since the carcass should not be wetted. If it has to be washed, it must be thoroughly drained and dried.

Mix together the ingredients for the marinade and rub it on the lamb, both inside and out.

Cut slits in the flesh with a long pointed knife, and insert the slivers of shallots and garlic. Put the liver (if not used earlier for breakfast), heart and kidneys inside the carcass, and leave it to rest on a large tray for 2 hours.

Tie the feet firmly together and jam the head between the legs. Hang the carcass up by the feet on a strong iron spit, fastening it to the spit with an additional loop of wire around the middle to prevent it from falling into the fire.

When the fire in the pit dies down and is glowing steadily, set on top of it a large pan half full of water for the lamb's juices to drip into. Lower the spit into position in the tandır so that the entire animal is hanging inside the pit. Cover the open top of the tandır with a firm wire mesh plastered with mud to seal the oven. Seal the air vent under the tandır in the same way. Leave the çebiç to cook; the time obviously depends on the age and size of the animal. A young, lean animal takes 1–1½ hours; a fat, older one 2½–3½ hours. While it is cooking, check the tandır from time to time and seal any holes that develop with mud.

When the meat is ready, tap the edges of the wire mesh to break the mud seal, remove the mesh and lift the spit out of the pit by the ends. Untie the animal from the spit, free its head from between its legs and put it on a tray. Remove the heart and kidneys, chop them and add to the juices collected in the pan at the bottom of the tandır. Cover the meat to keep it warm. Cook the bulgur pilaf quickly in the pan over the dying embers (p.121).

Spread the pilaf on a tray large enough to take the lamb, put the lamb on top of it, and put the parsley soaked in onion juice in its mouth.

◊ KIŞ KAĞIT KEBABI ◊

WINTER KEBAB IN PAPER PARCELS

TO SERVE 4
½ portion of upside-down kebab (p.62)
250g/8oz carrots, scraped
250g/8oz potatoes, peeled
sunflower oil for deep-frying
250g/8oz cooked peas
25g/1oz dill, finely chopped
4 × 35cm/14 inch squares of greaseproof paper

Cook the meat as for upside-down kebab (p.62), strain off the liquid and reserve.

Parboil the carrots, strain and dice into 2.5cm/1 inch cubes. Cut the potatoes to the same size. Fry the potatoes, then the carrots in very hot sunflower oil and drain well.

Mix the vegetables with the meat and divide into four portions. Put one portion on each piece of greaseproof, pour over a spoonful of the kebab liquid and sprinkle with the chopped dill. Wrap up the parcels, twist the ends and tuck them underneath. Place the packets on a baking tray. Brush with water and cook in a preheated oven for 15 minutes at 250°C/500°F/gas mark 10.

Place the kebabs on a serving dish, cut off the top of each paper parcel and serve hot.

◊ TAS KEBABI ◊
UPSIDE-DOWN KEBAB

Stewed dishes occupy an important place in Turkish cuisine. One of the best known of these dishes is tas kebabı. This is prepared in various parts of Turkey in a variety of ways. Tas kebabı with pilaf is so popular it is practically a national dish.

TO SERVE 4–6
1kg/2lb shoulder or leg of lamb
25g/1oz cooking fat or butter
300g/10oz onions, finely chopped
25g/1oz tomato purée
1tsp red pepper
¼tsp ground black pepper
¼tsp ground cinnamon
¼tsp dried thyme
1 small bay leaf
1L/1¾ pints meat stock (p.33) or water
1tbsp vinegar
salt to taste
ACCOMPANIMENT
rice pilaf made with 250g/8oz rice

Chop the meat into 3cm/1½ inch cubes and put in a pan on medium heat. Shake the pan until the meat has browned and absorbed its own juices, then add the fat and onions and fry for 3–4 minutes, stirring, until the onions are golden. Add the tomato purée and stir for another minute. Add the spices and herbs. Pour on the boiling stock and add the vinegar. Cover the pan. When it comes to the boil simmer for 1½–2 hours until the meat is tender. Add salt and after 5 minutes remove from the heat.

Strain the meat. Reserve the liquid and put the meat in an earthenware bowl. Place the bowl upside down in the middle of a large pan. Top up the liquid to 500ml/17fl oz. Place the rice, already washed and soaked in salty water, in the pan around the bowl, add the boiling hot liquid and cover the pan. Cook over medium heat and when the rice is ready, bring the pan to the table, lift off the bowl and serve hot.

That is how this dish came to be known as pilaf with upside-down kebab.

◊ DOMALANLI ŞİŞ KEBABI ◊
KEBAB WITH TRUFFLES

TO SERVE 6
1 quantity şiş kebab (p.57)
250g/8oz truffles (p.81)
FOR THE GARNISH
slices of tomato and peppers
ACCOMPANIMENTS
bulgur pilaf (p.121) or
firik (roasted unripe wheat, p.122)
cucumber cacık (p.114)

Prepare the şiş kebab.

Peel the truffles and cut them into pieces of the same size as the meat cubes. Pierce the truffle pieces through the middle with a sharp pointed knife. If you try to skewer them without piercing them first, they will tear. Thread the skewers alternately with two pieces of meat and one piece of truffle. Grill over a charcoal fire and serve garnished with slices of tomato and peppers, with bulgur pilaf or firik, and cucumber cacık.

◊ ISLIM KEBABI ◊

S T E A M E D   K E B A B S

TO SERVE 4
1 portion upside-down kebab (p.62)
500g/1lb aubergines
salt
sunflower oil for deep frying
300g/10oz medium tomatoes
3 large peppers
6 toothpicks
A C C O M P A N I M E N T
cacık (p.114)

Make the upside-down kebab as described on p.62. When sufficiently cool, strain and keep the liquid.

Peel the aubergines, slice thickly lengthways, sprinkle with salt and leave for 1 hour. Wash them thoroughly, drain and dry. Fry in hot oil for 2 minutes, then lay out on absorbent paper.

Thickly slice the tomatoes from the top.

Cut the peppers in half or in three depending on their size.

Line 4 teacups with 2 or three slices of aubergine, leaving the ends of the slices hanging over the edge. Put an equal amount of cooked meat in each cup, press it down firmly, and fold the ends of the aubergine slices over the meat. Put a slice of tomato on top and deposit the contents of each cup in a wide-bottomed casserole or pan by turning them over. Place another tomato slice and a slice of pepper on top and pin down with a toothpick. Pour the reserved meat liquid gently down the side of the pan, taking care not to disturb the kebabs. Cover the pan and cook on very low heat for 10–15 minutes. Serve hot.

NOTE: Islim kebabs may also be cooked, covered, in a low oven for 40 minutes and for a final 5 minutes uncovered. Hasan paşa köftesi (p.72), fried in a little butter may be used instead of upside-down kebab.

◊ HÜNKAR BEĞENDI ◊

S U L T A N ' S   R E L I S H   K E B A B

TO SERVE 6	
1 portion upside-down kebab (p.62)	*1tbsp salt*
500ml/17fl oz milk	*1L/1¾ pints water*
1kg/2lb aubergines	
100g/3½oz butter	
50g/2oz flour	
salt to taste	
50g/2oz kaşar cheese (p.173), grated	
FOR THE MARINADE	
2tbsp lemon juice	

Cook the meat as described on p.62. Meanwhile, boil and cool the milk. Mix together the ingredients for the marinade. Pierce the skin of the aubergines in several places with a knife and cook until tender, either directly over a coal fire or in the oven at 250°C/500°F/gas mark 10. They should take about 30 minutes. When cool enough to touch, remove the skin and marinate for

20 minutes until the flesh turns white. Drain well, place in a bowl and mash with a wooden pestle or spoon, or purée in a food processor.

Melt the butter in a pan, stir in the flour and cook, stirring, for 2 minutes to make a roux. Remove from the heat and beat in the aubergine purée with a wooden spoon. Stir in the cooled milk, bring to the boil, add salt, replace on the heat and cook for about 2 minutes, stirring all the time until the mixture has the consistency of yoghurt. Add the cheese, stir until incorporated, then remove from the heat.

Put the upside-down kebab meat in the middle of a heated serving dish and the aubergine purée around the meat. Serve hot.

◊ KAĞITTA KUZU PIRZOLASI ◊

LAMB CHOPS EN PAPILLOTE

TO SERVE 6
12 small chops
1tsp salt
1tsp dried thyme
50g/2oz cooking fat or butter
a few sprigs of parsley, chopped
6 × 35cm/14 inch squares greaseproof paper
FOR THE SAUCE
200g/7oz onions, chopped
25g/1oz green pepper, chopped
2 cloves garlic, chopped
400g/14oz tomatoes, peeled and chopped
¼tsp dried thyme
¼tsp red pepper
¼tsp ground cinnamon
salt to taste
100ml/3½fl oz meat stock

Sprinkle the chops with salt and thyme. Heat the fat and fry the chops on a very low heat for 4 minutes each side; remove to a plate.

Put the pan back on the heat and fry the onions for 7–8 minutes, add the peppers and fry for another 4 minutes. Add the garlic and tomatoes and fry for a further 5 minutes. Now put in the herbs, spices, salt and stock and cover the pan. Bring to the boil, then cook on very low heat for 10 minutes until the onions are very soft.

Grease each piece of paper with butter and put two chops on top of each other in the centre of each. Divide the vegetable mixture between the chops. Sprinkle with parsley. Fold the paper over and make firm, secure parcels. Put the parcels in a large oven dish and brush over with water. Cook in the oven at 200°C/400°F/gas mark 6, for 15 minutes.

Place the parcels on a serving dish, cut off the top half of the paper and serve hot.

◊ ŞİŞ KÖFTE ◊

KÖFTE ON SKEWERS

Good şiş köfte should fall apart at the touch of a fork, and to achieve this the meat should be finely chopped by hand.

TO SERVE 2–3
300g/10oz leg of lamb
200g/7oz tail or other fat
salt
red pepper
1kg/2lb tomatoes, halved
basting liquid (p.57)
A C C O M P A N I M E N T S
cacık (p.114)
bulgur pilaf (p.119)
broad-bladed metal skewers

Remove the sinewy parts of the meat. Chop the meat and fat finely with a cleaver. Add salt and pepper to taste and knead it in well. Divide into six portions and fix each portion on a skewer by squashing the skewer into the minced meat in the palm of your hand.

Grill the tomatoes until tender. Crush with a pestle in a bowl to make a pulp, remove the skins, and transfer to a serving dish.

Position the skewers 10cm/4 inches above a charcoal fire and grill for 4–6 minutes, turning and basting as necessary.

Draw the köfte off the skewers, place them on top of the tomato pulp, and serve immediately with cacık and bulgur pilaf.

◊ CIZBIZ ◊

GRILLED MEATBALLS

Cızbız is a type of meatball popular throughout Turkey. It is often cut into four and tucked with chopped onion salad into a large roll. Sold everywhere by street traders and called Köfte-Ekmek, this is the Turkish version of fast food.

TO SERVE 2
250g/8oz minced leg of lamb
100g/3½oz onions, grated
a few sprigs parsley, finely chopped
½tsp salt
½tsp black pepper
½tsp dried thyme

¼tsp cinnamon
¼tsp red pepper
1 quantity basting liquor (p.57)
ACCOMPANIMENT
onion or any other kind of salad

Place the minced meat in a bowl, and add all the other ingredients. Knead well for 5–10 minutes, then divide into oval balls.

Place the meatballs (köfte) on a wire grill and position it 10cm/4 inches above a charcoal fire. Grill for 4–6 minutes, turning and basting as necessary.

Serve in a preheated serving dish while hot, together with a salad.

◊ KURU KÖFTE ◊

DRY KÖFTE

These köfte, or rissoles, can be kept for a long time, and are frequently taken on picnics and long journeys.

TO SERVE 6
500g/1lb leg of lamb, minced
100g/3½oz onions
50g/2oz stale breadcrumbs
2tbsp finely chopped parsley
1 egg, beaten
1tsp salt
1tsp red pepper
1tsp ground black pepper
¼tsp ground cinnamon
¼tsp ground cumin
¼tsp ground allspice
¼tsp dried thyme

150g/5oz cooking fat or olive oil for frying
25g/1oz plain flour
ACCOMPANIMENT
fried potatoes

Mince the meat once more so it is very smooth. Grate the onions over the meat and stir in the breadcrumbs and parsley. Add the egg, salt, spices and thyme and knead the mixture for about 10 minutes. Make the köfte in the shape of a cigar, about the length and thickness of your index finger.

Heat the fat or oil in a frying pan. Spread the flour on a large plate. Roll the köfte in flour and fry for 10 minutes, gently shaking the pan to ensure they are cooked on all sides.

◊ SAÇTA SUCUK KÖFTE ◊

GARLIC KÖFTE IN TOMATO SAUCE

TO SERVE 6
500g/1lb leg of lamb, minced twice
6–8 cloves garlic
1tsp salt
½tsp red pepper
½tsp ground black pepper
½tsp ground cumin
¼tsp ground cinnamon
¼tsp ground allspice
25g/1oz cooking fat or butter
FOR THE SAUCE
600g/1¼lb tomatoes or 25g/1oz tomato purée and 200ml/7fl oz water
ACCOMPANIMENTS
couscous pilaf cooked with tomatoes (p.124)
ayran (p.168)

Crush the garlic with the salt, and add to the meat with the spices. Knead for 5 minutes and prepare köfte the size of your little finger.

Place a pan on the heat and add half the fat. Put in the köfte and fry on each side for 4 minutes. Remove from the pan and keep warm.

Now make the sauce. Peel, deseed and grate the tomatoes. Put the remaining fat in the pan and add the tomato pulp. Cook for about 10 minutes, uncovered, until the tomatoes absorb their juices. (If using tomato purée, put it in the pan and stir for 1 minute, then add the water, and boil until the liquid reduces and thickens.) Add the köfte to the sauce and keep turning for 1 minute.

Transfer to a heated serving dish and serve with couscous and ayran, or for a picnic use the köfte as a filling for pitta bread.

◊ KADINBUDU KÖFTE ◊

LADY'S THIGH KÖFTE

TO SERVE 4
25g/1oz rice
salt
25g/1oz butter
50g/2oz onions, finely chopped
250g/8oz leg of lamb, minced twice
1tsp ground black pepper
1tsp ground cinnamon
3 eggs
250g/8oz cooking fat or olive oil for frying
50g/2oz plain flour or fine breadcrumbs

ACCOMPANIMENT
ayran (p.168)

Wash the rice. Bring 250ml/8fl oz water to the boil with 1tsp salt, turn off, add the rice and leave for 5 minutes.

Melt the butter on medium heat, add the onions and fry for 5 minutes. Drain the rice, add it to the onions and fry for 2 minutes. Add 50ml/2fl oz water and ¼tsp salt, bring to the boil, then cover the pan, and simmer gently for 5 minutes until the liquid is absorbed. Leave to cool.

Place half of the meat in a dry pan, cover and cook for about 5 minutes, stirring occasionally, until the meat absorbs its juices. Remove from the heat and mix the raw mince into the cooked meat. Add the rice and onion, pepper, half the cinnamon and a further ½ tsp salt. Mix in 1 egg and knead for 5 minutes. Divide into 12 portions the size of an egg, and flatten them to an oval shape.

Whisk the remaining eggs thoroughly in a small bowl. Heat the fat or oil in a frying pan. Spread the flour or breadcrumbs on a large plate. Roll the köfte in flour first, then dip in egg and place in the hot oil. Reduce the heat and fry for 2 minutes each side until the köfte are golden. Transfer to a saucepan, cover tightly and leave them to stand in their own steam for 5 minutes.

Place on a heated serving dish, sprinkle with the remaining cinnamon and serve.

◊ SALÇALI KÖFTE ◊

KÖFTE IN SAUCE

TO SERVE 6–8
500g/1lb leg of lamb, minced twice
200g/7oz onions
20g/³⁄₄oz chopped parsley
1tsp salt
½tsp ground black pepper
½tsp dried thyme
¼tsp ground cinnamon
¼tsp ground allspice
½tsp ground cumin
FOR THE VEGETABLES
500g/1lb potatoes, peeled and sliced
1 medium tomato
2–3 thin green peppers, sliced or cut in chunks
FOR THE SAUCE
25g/1oz cooking fat or butter
200g/7oz tomatoes, peeled and grated
2 cloves garlic, crushed
1 small bay leaf
½tsp salt or to taste
200ml/7fl oz water
30cm/12 inch diameter shallow casserole

Put the meat in a bowl, grate the onions over it, mix in the parsley and seasonings and knead for 5 minutes. Divide into equal portions the size of an egg, roll and flatten into oval köfte.

To make the sauce, melt the cooking fat or butter in a pan, add the tomatoes and stir for 1 minute. Add the garlic, bay leaf, salt and water, cover the pan, bring to the boil and remove from the heat after 1 minute.

Grease the casserole, put a layer of potato slices in the bottom and on top a layer of köfte. Cut the tomato in half and place in the middle; put the peppers between the köfte. Put on the lid and bake for 5 minutes in a preheated oven at 250°C/500°F/gas mark 10. Add the sauce and cook for a further 50–60 minutes until the potatoes and köfte are tender. Serve from the casserole.

◊ IÇLI KÖFTE ◊
MOTHER-IN-LAW'S KÖFTES

Içli köfte is a common dish throughout southeastern Anatolia. In Adiyaman, when a bride comes to her new home, her mother-in-law leaves whatever she intended doing after the noon prayers to prepare içli köfte. She hollows out the köfte, stuffs in a filling and seals up the hole, thinking to herself: "may the bride's mouth be sealed likewise"! She cooks them hoping that her daughter-in-law will not be too talkative and will prove an obedient wife. The bride and her husband eat mother-in-law's köfte the following day.

TO SERVE 6
FOR THE FILLING
25g/1oz cooking fat
100g/3½oz onions, finely chopped
125g/4oz minced lamb
25g/1oz shelled walnuts
¼tsp salt or to taste
¼tsp dried thyme
¼tsp red pepper
¼tsp ground black pepper
¼tsp ground cinnamon
¼tsp ground cumin
¼tsp ground allspice
2tbsp chopped parsley
FOR THE KÖFTE
125g/4oz minced lamb
150g/5oz finely ground bulgur
1tbsp coriander seeds
¼tsp each salt and red pepper
250g/8oz cooking fat or olive oil for deep frying
ACCOMPANIMENT
radish and tahina salad (p.113)

To make the filling, melt the fat in a frying pan on medium heat, add the onions and fry for about 5 minutes until golden. Add the mince and fry for approximately 7–8 minutes, stirring constantly, until the meat has absorbed its juices. Chop the walnuts with a knife without crumbling them (do not crush in a mortar), add to the meat with the salt, thyme and spices, stir and remove from the heat. Sprinkle on the parsley and allow to cool. The filling can be prepared a day in advance and kept in the fridge.

To prepare the köfte, place the bulgur in a shallow bowl. Grind or pound the coriander and add with the salt and red pepper. Knead the bulgur with pressing movements for 30 minutes, or work in a food processor, adding a little hot water from time to time, but no more than 150ml/ ¼ pint. When the bulgur has become doughy add the minced meat. Knead for another 10–15 minutes, or process further until the meat and bulgur are well mixed and stick together like dough.

Divide the paste into portions the size of an egg. Normally this quantity should make 18 köfte. Hold each one in the palm of the hand and with the index finger hollow it out to form a shell, like an empty eggshell. Stuff with the cold filling and seal the hole by pinching the top with a twisting movement.

When the köfte are ready, heat the fat or oil and fry for 3–4 minutes, turning them over. Remove and drain on absorbent paper. The köfte may be eaten hot or cold.
NOTE: If you have difficulty in getting the köfte mixture to bind, add 1tbsp of flour.

◊ ÇIĞ KÖFTE ◊
RAW KÖFTES

According to a popular folk song, "Raw köfte are very hot, Ayran is the right antidotal shot!" Raw köfte are a speciality in southeastern Anatolia. What is special about them is that they are highly spiced and very hot indeed. The inhabitants of Şanlı Urfa believe that really hot dishes improve the voice!

TO SERVE 6
2tbsp chilli flakes
100ml/3½fl oz water
250g/8oz leg of very fresh prime quality lamb
250g/8oz finely ground bulgur
25g/1oz tomato purée
2 cloves garlic, crushed
½tsp ground cumin
½tsp ground black pepper
½tsp ground cinnamon
½tsp ground allspice
½tsp ground cloves
¼tsp ground ginger
1tsp salt
100g/3½oz spring onions, finely chopped
small bunch of parsley, finely chopped
ACCOMPANIMENTS
pomegranate syrup (p.173) or minced meat with eggs (p.45)
ayran (p.168)

Soak the chilli flakes in the water for 30 minutes. Cut away any sinewy parts from the meat and tenderize with a wooden mallet on a marble slab before mincing, or mince twice, or chop in a food processor until very smooth. Put the meat and bulgur in a bowl, add the tomato purée, garlic and seasonings. Knead thoroughly until all the ingredients stick together, dipping your hands into hot water from time to time if necessary. (The art is to knead the mixture to the right consistency *without* wetting the hands.) When you can squeeze the mixture in the palm of the hand to form a meatball, add the onions and parsley and knead again until they are properly mixed in. Make into meatballs.

Serve the köfte without delay – they must be eaten before the bulgur swells up. Dip them in pomegranate syrup or eat with minced meat with eggs. The ayran provides the antidote.

◊ HASAN PAŞA KÖFTESI ◊

HASAN PASHA KÖFTE

In Ottoman times, delicious dishes comparable to those of the imperial palaces were produced for banquets in the homes of ministers, religious dignitaries and noblemen. Cooks were always trying to devise new dishes. Hasan paşa köftesi was named after the pasha whose cooks conceived the recipe. It is a delicious köfte contrived for guests who shy away from rich food.

TO SERVE 6
250g/8oz leg of lamb, minced
25g/1oz breadcrumbs
100g/3½oz onions, grated
1 egg
¼tsp dried thyme
¼tsp salt
¼tsp red pepper
¼tsp ground black pepper
¼tsp ground cumin
¼tsp ground cinnamon
¼tsp ground allspice
25g/1oz cooking fat or butter
150ml/¼ pint meat stock (p.33)
1 bay leaf
25g/1oz tomato purée
FOR THE POTATO PURÉE
500g/1lb potatoes, peeled
25g/1oz butter
1 egg
150ml/¼ pint hot milk
¼tsp grated nutmeg
¼tsp salt or to taste
ACCOMPANIMENT
vermicelli

To make the purée, boil the potatoes and purée through a sieve or vegetable mill into a pan. Add the butter, egg, milk, nutmeg and salt. Whisk to a smooth purée over medium heat. Remove from the heat, and once the potato has stopped bubbling, transfer it to a piping bag, if you have one.

To make the köfte, mince or grind the meat once more. Put the breadcrumbs through a sieve.

In a large bowl knead together the mince, breadcrumbs, onions, egg, thyme, salt and spices for 10 minutes, roll into balls and shape into small cups. Grease a 20cm/8 inch casserole with some of the cooking fat or butter. Put in the köfte. Divide the remaining butter between the hollows of each köfte and cook for 20 minutes in a preheated oven at 200°C/400°F/gas mark 6. Bring the meat stock to the boil, crumble in the bay leaf and add half the tomato purée. Cover and simmer for 5 minutes.

Remove the köfte from the oven and fill the hollows with potato purée, using a spoon if you have no piping bag. Top with a small drop of tomato purée, to use up the remainder.

Pour the hot stock around the köfte. Return to the oven at 200°C/400°F/gas mark 6, for about 10 minutes until the potato purée turns golden brown.

Serve hot with vermicelli.

◊ TERBIYELI KUZU KAPAMASI ◊

LAMB FRICASSÉE

TO SERVE 6
6 chump chops or leg cutlets
100g/3½oz spring onions, cut into 4cm/1½ inch lengths
100g/3½oz carrots, peeled and cut into 4cm/1½ inch lengths
6 cos lettuce leaves, chopped
2tbsp chopped mint
2tbsp chopped parsley
1tsp each salt and sugar
1 egg yolk
1tbsp each flour and lemon juice
ACCOMPANIMENTS
couscous pilaf with tomato sauce (p.124)

Put the meat in a pan with 750ml/1¼ pints hot water, bring to the boil and skim off any scum. Add the vegetables, herbs, salt and sugar; cover and simmer for 1–1½ hours until the meat is tender.

In a bowl whisk together the egg yolk, flour and lemon juice. Pour a ladleful of liquid from the stew into the mixture, whisking well, then slowly pour it back into the stew, stirring briskly. Simmer for 1 minute. Serve at once with couscous pilaf and tomato sauce.

◊ ELBASAN TAVASI ◊

LAMB CHOPS IN YOGHURT SAUCE

TO SERVE 5–6
5–6 loin chops
vegetable ingredients for meat stock (p.33)
salt to taste
FOR THE SAUCE
1kg/2lb thick-set yoghurt
50g/2oz flour
2 egg yolks
ACCOMPANIMENT
pilaf of firik – roasted unripe wheat (p.122)

Put the chops in a heavy pan and brown them without fat for 4–5 minutes until the juices are absorbed. Add the vegetables and water to cover. Cover the pan and cook for 1–1½ hours until the meat is really tender. Add salt, remove from the heat after 5 minutes, and lift out the meat.

Whisk the yoghurt and flour thoroughly in a small saucepan. Add the egg yolks and whisk again.

Place the chops in an oven dish that will hold them in one layer and pour over the yoghurt mixture. Bake, uncovered, in a preheated oven at 250°C/500°F/gas mark 10, for 25–30 minutes until the surface is golden brown. Serve hot in the pan.

◊ NOHUTLU YAHNI ◊

MUTTON STEW WITH CHICKPEAS

This stew can be served on croûtons if the tomato purée is omitted. Cut slices of bread into 2cm/¾ inch squares and "bake" briefly in the oven. Pour the stew over the bread and serve.

TO SERVE 6
6 single or 3 double loin chops
150g/5oz chickpeas, soaked overnight
1tsp salt
25g/1oz cooking fat
25g/1oz tomato purée (optional)
150g/5oz small onions, quartered
ACCOMPANIMENTS
rice pilaf (p.119)
zerde (p.149)

Drain the chickpeas and boil in 1.5L/2½ pints fresh water for about 1 hour until they are semi-tender. Drain.

Put the meat in a pan with 1L/1¾ pints of hot water. Bring to the boil, remove any scum, cover the pan and cook for 1 hour on low heat. Add the salt. If the liquid has reduced, top up with hot water.

Melt the fat in a small frying pan. Fry the onions on low heat for 4 minutes, add the tomato purée if using and add to the meat with the chickpeas. Cook on very low heat for about 1 hour until both peas and meat are really tender.

Taste for seasoning and add more salt if necessary. Remove from the heat after a further 5 minutes and serve the stew with rice pilaf and zerde.

◊ KELLE-PAÇA ◊

SHEEP'S HEAD AND TROTTER SOUP

If a sheep's head is served whole, the meat is eaten, then the brain is extracted and and offered first to a guest or to the head of the household, and then passed round for others to help themselves.

Cold sheep's head has become so popular that you will find it being sold on street corners and at railway stations in every Anatolian town. In Diyarbakır in south-eastern Anatolia the menfolk usually have a dish of hot sheep's head and trotters for breakfast at the market before starting work.

TO SERVE 6–8
1 skinned sheep's head
6 skinned trotters
100g/3½oz onions, quartered
small bunch parsley
2 bay leaves
4L/7 pints water
salt to taste
8 cloves of garlic
50ml/2fl oz vinegar or lemon juice
FOR THE SAUCE
50g/2oz suet, chopped
1tbsp onion juice (p.48)
50g/2oz lamb, finely chopped
1 marrow bone, cracked into 3
2 cloves
1.25cm/½ inch stick of cinnamon
1tsp red pepper

Split open the jaw and thoroughly clean the snout by hitting it on a marble slab. Immerse the head in plenty of water in a bowl and soak for 1 hour. Repeat the cleaning and washing process and place the head in a pan.

Wash the trotters thoroughly and add them to the pan, with the onions, parsley and bay leaves. Fill it up with cold water. Bring to the boil and skim off the scum, then cover and simmer on very low heat for 10–12 hours until the meat from the head and trotters comes off the bone. (If using a pressure cooker, cook for 1 hour.)

Strain the cooking liquid into a clean pan and reserve. Remove the meat from the bones, return to the cooking liquid and bring to the boil. Add salt to taste. Cook for 10 minutes.

Crush the garlic with the vinegar or lemon juice. Stir into the soup and pour into a soup tureen.

For the sauce, render the suet in a small pan. Add the onion juice, lamb, marrow bone, cloves and cinnamon. Fry until the meat is well cooked. Strain off the fat, add the red pepper, cook for 1 minute then remove from the heat. When the pepper settles at the bottom, strain off the fat and pour it thinly over the surface of the soup.

◊ BUMBAR DOLMASI ◊

LIVER SAUSAGE

Bumbar is very popular in southeastern Anatolia. In Siirt they even hold an annual three-day Bumbar Festival. On the first Monday in February, when narcissi – the first flowers of spring – are gathered on the mountains and hilltops, it is customary to make a particular kind of bumbar known as "cokat" and to eat it with a compote of grapes and apricots. Prospective mothers-in-law send their sons' fiancées presents, including bumbar, baklava and fruit. The future mother-in-law does this only while the girl is engaged; once married the daughter-in-law is obliged, as with the Egg Festival, to present her mother-in-law annually with gifts of bumbar and other presents for the rest of her life.

Mince the liver. Wash the rice and add to the liver with the spices, 1tsp salt and 2 tbsp water. Mix well.

Tie one end of the gut. Insert a wide-bottomed funnel at the other end and fill the gut; tie the end. Place in a pan with 1L/1¾ pints salted water. Bring to the boil, skim off the scum, cover the pan and lower the heat. After about 15 minutes prick the bumbar in several places with a pin. (If pricked earlier, the stuffing would cook while the skin remained uncooked.) Simmer for 15–25 minutes more, until the bumbar is tender. Drain off the water, place a cloth or absorbent paper between the pan and the lid and leave for 15 minutes.

Place the bumbar on a heated serving dish and serve hot with the compote.

TO SERVE 6
2 large guts suitable for stuffing, or large sausage casings
salt
200ml/7fl oz vinegar
FOR THE SAUSAGE
250g/8oz liver
100g/3½oz rice
½tsp ground black pepper
½tsp red pepper
¼tsp ground cinnamon
¼tsp ground cumin
¼tsp ground allspice
salt
ACCOMPANIMENT
compote of dried apricots and grapes

Thoroughly clean the inside and outside of the gut by rubbing with salt. Soak in vinegar for 1 hour then wash thoroughly.

◊ DÜĞÜN YAHNISI ◊

WEDDING STEW

Düğün yahnisi is the traditional dish to serve at wedding receptions.

TO SERVE 6
6 loin chops
1L/1¾ pints water
50g/2oz butter
200g/7oz onions, sliced
1.25cm/½ inch cinnamon stick
2 cloves
½tsp salt
FOR THE GARNISH
2tbsp chopped parsley
ACCOMPANIMENT
rice pilaf (p.119)

Put the meat and water in a pan and bring to the boil. Skim off any scum and lift out the chops. Reserve the liquid.

Melt the butter and fry the chops on low heat for 2 minutes on each side, then return them to the liquid in the pan. In the butter left in the frying pan sweat the onions for 4 minutes, then add with the butter to the meat. Add the cinnamon and cloves, bring to the boil and then simmer on very low heat for 1–1½ hours until the meat is really tender. Add salt and cook for another 5 minutes.

Place on a serving dish, sprinkle with parsley and serve hot with rice pilaf.

◊ ARNAVUT CIĞERI ◊

ALBANIAN LIVER

TO SERVE 4–6
1 lamb's liver
1tbsp red pepper
50g/2oz plain flour
olive oil for deep-frying
1tsp salt
FOR THE GARNISH
3 sprigs parsley
1 tomato, sliced
ACCOMPANIMENT
onion salad (p.117)

coat the chopped liver on all sides. (To get rid of excess flour put the liver in a sieve and shake.) Heat the oil and fry for 2 minutes. Transfer the liver to an oven dish, sprinkle with salt and pour over 1tbsp oil from the frying pan. Place in a preheated oven at 200°C/400°F/gas mark 6, for 2 minutes, or cover the pan and put on the heat for 2 minutes, then turn off the heat and leave to stand for a further 5 minutes, to cook in its own steam.

Garnish with parsley and slices of tomato, and serve with an onion salad.

Skin the liver, cut in small cubes, wash and drain thoroughly. Sprinkle on the red pepper, spread the flour on a flat dish, and

◊ PATLICANLI BILDIRCIN ◊

QUAILS NESTLING IN AUBERGINES

"And we caused clouds to shade you and manna and quails to descend upon you, saying: 'Eat of the good things which we have given you for food'."

(THE KORAN, CHAPTER II, "THE COW", VERSE 57)

TO SERVE 4
4 quails
4 large plump aubergines
salt
200ml/7fl oz sunflower oil
50g/2oz onions, sliced
25g/1oz mild green chilli, chopped
300g/10oz tomatoes
1 large pepper
200ml/7fl oz boiling water
4 toothpicks

Peel the aubergines in alternate strips. Cut in half lengthways. Carefully hollow out as much flesh as possible. Reserve it for another dish. Sprinkle with salt, leave for 20 minutes, then rinse and drain.

Heat the oil and fry both sides of the aubergines for 2–3 minutes. Remove and drain.

Add the quails to the pan and sauté both sides for 8 minutes.

Leave 1tbsp of fat in the pan and pour off the rest. Fry the onions for 3 minutes until golden, add the chilli and stir for 1 minute. Set aside one tomato, peel and chop the rest, and add to the pan. Stir for 3–4 minutes, then remove from the heat.

Spread the tomato mixture in a baking dish, place four aubergine halves on the mixture, place a quail in each and cover with the remaining aubergine halves.

Cut the remaining tomato and the large pepper in 4 slices. Place a slice of each – tomato first and pepper next – on top of the aubergines and secure with a toothpick. Sprinkle with salt.

Pour on the boiling water. Cover the dish and bake in a preheated oven at 200°C/ 400°F/gas mark 6, for 40 minutes and for 5 minutes, uncovered, at the end.

Serve hot straight from the oven.

79

◊ YUFKALI PILIÇ ◊
POUSSIN IN A CRUST

MAKES 4 PASTIES
400g/14oz poussin
25g/1oz butter
75g/3oz onions, finely sliced
25g/1oz thin green peppers, finely chopped
200g/7oz tomatoes, peeled and chopped
1tsp salt or to taste
100ml/3½fl oz hot water
FOR THE CRUST
2 sheets of yufka (wafer-thin dough, p.59)
25g/1oz melted butter

Put the poussin in a heavy covered pan and cook for about 10–15 minutes on low heat until the released juices are absorbed. When it begins to sizzle, remove from the pan. To the same pan add the butter and cook the onions for 3–4 minutes until golden. Add the peppers and stir for 1 minute. Add the tomatoes and stir for 4–5 minutes.

Place the poussin in the pan once again, add the salt and water and cover the pan. When it begins to boil, lower the heat and cook for about 40 minutes, until the poussin is tender. Leave to cool in the pan.

Remove the meat from the bones and cut into small pieces. Stir the meat into the tomato mixture.

Divide the yufka in half. Brush with a little melted butter. Divide the filling between them and fold over the four corners, envelope fashion. Place in a greased baking dish and brush over with melted butter. Bake in a preheated oven at 250°C/500°F/gas mark 10, for about 5 minutes, until the yufka are pale gold.

◊ GÜVEÇTE TAVŞAN YAHNISI ◊
RABBIT CASSEROLE

Furred game is not eaten much by Moslem Turks, because the animal is not killed in accordance with religious requirements. Nevertheless rabbit or hare is the favourite catch of keen hunters. This stew could also be prepared in small single-portion earthenware cooking pots.

TO SERVE 4
1kg/2lb rabbit meat
200ml/7fl oz water
200ml/7fl oz vinegar
100g/3½oz cooking fat or butter
300g/10oz onions, finely chopped
10 whole cloves of garlic
25g/1oz tomato purée
25g/1oz parsley, chopped
500ml/17fl oz meat stock (p.33)
25ml/1fl oz vinegar
1 small bay leaf
½tsp ground black pepper
½tsp red pepper
½tsp dried thyme
salt to taste
ACCOMPANIMENT
couscous

Cut the rabbit into four portions and soak in the water and vinegar for 24 hours. Wash and drain.

Melt the fat in a casserole, and fry the rabbit for about 10 minutes, turning the pieces occasionally, until the meat soaks up all its juices. Add the onions and garlic and fry for 10 minutes; add the tomato purée and stir for 2 minutes, then add the parsley. Pour over the meat stock and vinegar, add the seasoning, cover the pan and stew on very low heat for about 2 hours, until the meat is tender. Serve hot in the casserole (güveç) with a dish of couscous.

◊ DOMALANLI PILIÇ GÜVECI ◊

CASSEROLE OF POUSSIN WITH TURKISH TRUFFLES

The best truffles in Turkey are to be found in central Anatolia in the Konya region. These truffles are very different from French or Italian truffles in taste. In the villages they are used as a meat substitute because they give a meaty flavour to the dish. They go well with rice, vegetables and kebabs and this pilaf made with truffles is particularly delicious.

TO SERVE 4
2 poussins of 400g/14oz each, cut into 4
50g/2oz butter
200g/7oz potatoes, peeled and diced
200g/7oz truffles peeled and sliced
50g/2oz onions, sliced into rings
25g/1oz small green pepper, finely chopped
200g/7oz tomatoes, peeled, deseeded and chopped
200ml/7fl oz water
1tsp salt
1tsp ground black pepper
ACCOMPANIMENT
bulgur pilaf (p.119)
ayran (p.168)

Melt the butter, add the poussins, fry for 5 minutes and transfer to a casserole. Add the potatoes and truffles to the pan, fry for 2 minutes and transfer to the casserole. Remove all but 1tbsp of fat from the frying pan before adding the onions and peppers. Fry for 2–3 minutes then add the tomatoes, stir for 3 minutes and transfer to the casserole. Add the water, season with salt and pepper, cover and put on the heat. When it comes to the boil, lower the heat and cook for 1 hour.

Serve in the casserole (güveç) with bulgur pilaf and ayran.

VEGETABLE AND FRUIT
DISHES WITH MEAT

◊ DOLMALAR ◊

STUFFED VEGETABLES

Dolmas, in their infinite variety, constitute an important part of Turkish cuisine. The stuffings may be of meat and vegetables, as in the two featured here from Istanbul; and in Anatolia they often include coarsely ground wheat (yarma).

In the south they insert cloves of garlic in dolmas to enhance the flavour. In some parts of south-eastern and eastern Anatolia they use sumac sauce or lemon salt to impart a bitter taste to the dish.

Marrow, quince and plum dolmas, stuffed with sweetmeat, rarely seen in Istanbul, appear regularly in central Anatolia and are a noted speciality of Konya.

In the section on dolmas and sarmas I have tried to provide a sample selection of each in the hope that they will prove to your liking. Note that a dolma is a container – usually a vegetable or fruit – into which a filling is put, whereas a sarma is something wrapped up, often in a vegetable leaf.

◊ DOLMA STUFFINGS ◊

MEAT STUFFING I

This stuffing comes from Istanbul.

350g/12oz fat lamb, minced
250g/8oz onions, thinly sliced
1tsp salt
5g/¹/₄oz parsley, chopped
5g/¹/₄oz dill, chopped
5g/¹/₄oz mint, chopped
100g/3¹/₂oz rice, washed
50g/2oz cooking fat or butter
¹/₂tsp ground black pepper
¹/₂tsp red pepper
50ml/2fl oz meat stock or water

Place the mince in a bowl with the onions and salt. Leave for 2 minutes, then knead well with the hands. Add the remaining ingredients to the mince and knead. Use the stuffing for different kinds of dolmas and sarmas.

MEAT STUFFING II

This is a variation on the Istanbul stuffing, used mostly in central Anatolia.

1 quantity dolma stuffing I
100g/3¹/₂oz tomatoes, peeled, deseeded and finely chopped
25g/1oz tomato purée

Prepare the first stuffing. Thoroughly mix in the tomatoes and tomato purée. Use for different kinds of dolmas and sarmas.

MEAT STUFFING III

This stuffing is widely used in eastern and southeastern Anatolia. It is particularly favoured for sarmas with beet leaves and vine leaves. Diluted sumac is added to impart a sour flavour to the dolmas.

125g/4oz lamb, minced
75g/3oz coarsely ground wheat
150g/5oz onions, finely chopped
1tsp salt
250g/8oz tomatoes, peeled and finely chopped
250g/8oz green peppers, finely chopped
15g/¹⁄₂oz parsley, chopped
1tsp tomato purée
25ml/1fl oz sunflower oil

1tsp red pepper
1tsp ground black pepper
1tsp sumac (p.173) or
¹⁄₄tsp lemon salt (p.173)
50ml/2fl oz water

Place the mince in a pan. Pick the wheat over, wash and add to the pan, with the onions and salt and knead until soft. Add the remaining ingredients and knead until thoroughly combined.

◊ PAZI SARMASI ◊

SARMA OF BEET LEAVES

TO SERVE 4
1 quantity dolma stuffing III (above)
750g/1¹⁄₂lb beet leaves
2L/3¹⁄₂ pints water
salt
25g/1oz butter
1tsp sumac (p.173) or
¹⁄₄tsp lemon salt (p.173)
250ml/8fl oz hot water

Prepare the stuffing. Trim the leaves and blanch them in a large pan of boiling salted water for 1 minute. Drain and plunge the leaves into a large bowl of cold water for 2–3 minutes, then strain.

Wrap small portions of stuffing in the beet leaves and arrange them in a shallow pan with handles on either side. Add the butter. Mix the sumac sauce or lemon salt with the water and pour over the sarmas. Put a plate on top to prevent them from coming undone. Cover the pan, and when it begins to boil, reduce to very low heat and cook for 35–40 minutes.

Serve hot.

◊ ASMA YAPRAĞI SARMASI ◊

SARMA OF VINE LEAVES

TO SERVE 4
2 quantities dolma stuffing I (p.83)
250g/8oz vine leaves, either fresh or preserved in brine
25ml/1fl oz lemon juice
400ml/14fl oz meat stock (p.33)
salt to taste
FOR THE SAUCE
25ml/1fl oz lemon juice
1 egg yolk

Prepare the dolma stuffing. Wash the fresh vine leaves, parboil for 4 minutes with the lemon juice in a large pan of boiling water. Drain the leaves, refresh them with cold water and strain. Leaves preserved in brine need parboiling for only 1 minute.

Place 4–5 leaves in the bottom of a pan. Reserve the same number of leaves for the top of the dish. Divide the stuffing between the remaining leaves and roll up. Arrange the sarmas neatly in the pan, cover with the reserved leaves. To prevent the sarmas from coming undone, place a plate over them. Pour on the meat stock and cook for 50–60 minutes on low heat until the sarmas are tender. If necessary, add salt and after 5 minutes remove from heat.

When they are ready to serve, whisk the lemon juice and egg yolk together, mix into it a little liquid from the cooking pan and pour the sauce over the sarmas. Serve hot.

NOTE: Instead of the egg and lemon juice sauce, you could serve yoghurt with garlic (p.172).

◊ BIBER DOLMASI ◊

STUFFED PEPPERS

TO SERVE 4
1 quantity dolma stuffing II (p.83)
25g/1oz cooking fat or butter
6 small–medium peppers suitable for stuffing
300ml/½ pint water
½tsp salt
200ml/7fl oz meat stock
ACCOMPANIMENT
cucumber cacık (p.114)

Prepare the stuffing. Melt the fat, add the stuffing and stir-fry for 2 minutes (the stuffing must remain half-cooked).

Trim the stalks of the peppers, wash them and parboil in salted water for 2 minutes. Strain. When slightly cooler, cut a slice from the top of each pepper to form a lid and carefully clean out the seeds and membranes. Stuff the peppers, replace their tops and set them upright in a pan. Pour in the meat stock and place a plate on top. Bring to the boil, lower the heat and cook for 30–40 minutes or until the peppers are tender.

Serve hot with cucumber cacık.

◊ KARNIYARIK ◊

BUTTERFLIED AUBERGINES

Karnıyarık means "split open", and this is a favourite dish during summer months. This recipe is from Istanbul; in Anatolia karnıyarık is prepared without the nuts and currants.

TO SERVE 4
4 medium aubergines
1tbsp salt
125g/4oz butter or vegetable oil for frying
FOR THE STUFFING
1tbsp butter
1tbsp pine nuts
50g/2oz onions, finely chopped
125g/4oz minced lamb
100g/3½oz tomatoes, peeled and diced
1tsp tomato purée
1tsp currants
¼tsp ground black pepper
¼tsp red pepper
¼tsp ground cinnamon
¼tsp ground allspice
TO FINISH
2 green peppers
1 glass hot water
ACCOMPANIMENTS
vermicelli pilaf (p.119)

Peel the aubergines completely or in alternate strips. Slice along the middle lengthways to open like a butterfly, rub with salt and leave for 20 minutes. Soak in water for 5 minutes and drain.

Fry both sides of the aubergines in the butter or oil for 5 minutes. Place in a shallow double-handled pan or baking dish, opening them out flat on their backs so they cover the bottom of the pan.

Fry the pine nuts in butter for 1 minute, add the onions and fry for 3–4 minutes. Add the mince and fry for a further 5–10 minutes until the meat absorbs its own juices. Put in the tomatoes and tomato purée and stir for 1 minute. Add the currants, spices and salt to taste, stir and remove from the heat.

Pile the stuffing on the aubergines. Slice the peppers lengthways and put them on top. Add the hot water, pouring it gently down the side of the pan, cover and cook on very low heat for about 1 hour, or in the oven with a lid for 40 minutes and uncovered for 5 minutes.

Serve hot in the cooking dish.

◊ TATLI ET KABAGI ◊

STUFFED SQUASH

Stuffed squash is a dolma of Konya origin. This version is sweetened, but it can also be prepared in a savoury form with diced meat and chickpeas. Both are delicious. The dish works well with butternut or pattypan squash.

TO SERVE 4
1 butternut squash, weighing about 500g/1lb
5–6 rose geranium leaves
150g/5oz caster sugar
FOR THE STUFFING
125g/4oz fat scrag end of neck of lamb, minced
50g/2oz rice
4 pieces of mastic (p.173)
1tbsp caster sugar
½tsp ground cinnamon
½tsp crushed cloves
¼tsp salt
50ml/2fl oz water

To make the stuffing, put the meat in a pan. Wash the rice. Crush the mastic thoroughly with the sugar, add to the meat with all the other ingredients and mix. Stir-fry for 4–5 minutes until the meat changes colour. Remove from the heat and cover the pan.

Peel the squash and cut off the top to form a lid. Scoop out the seeds with your fingers, and prick the sides with a knife in several places. Fill with the stuffing, cover with the "lid" and secure with toothpicks.

Cover the bottom of a tall-sided heavy pan that will just hold the squash with rose geranium leaves. Set the stuffed squash upright on them. Stir 2tbsps sugar into enough water to come just over halfway up the squash. Bring to the boil, reduce to very low heat and cook for 1–1½ hours.

When the squash is tender remove the "lid", pour into it half the remaining sugar, replace the lid and secure as before. Sprinkle the rest of the sugar over the squash. Cover the pan and cook for a further 15–20 minutes until the squash absorbs the sugar and turns golden.

Place the dolma carefully on a heated serving dish and serve hot.

◊ ENGINAR OTURTMASI ◊

STUFFED ARTICHOKES

Oturtmas are dishes prepared with vegetables which are rounded and can be hollowed out, such as artichokes, aubergines or potatoes, and which keep their shape when cooked. Oturtma means "made to sit upright".

TO SERVE 6
6 large artichokes
1 lemon
1tbsp salt
1tsp flour
500ml/17fl oz stock or water
20g/³⁄₄oz butter
25ml/1fl oz lemon juice
100g/3½oz tomatoes, sliced
FOR THE STUFFING
100g/3½oz lean minced lamb
20g/³⁄₄oz cooking fat or butter
100g/3½oz onions, finely chopped
100g/3½oz tomatoes, peeled, deseeded and chopped
¼tsp each salt and ground black pepper

Cut off the artichoke stalks and the outer leaves. Cut the lemon in half, dip in salt and rub the artichokes to prevent them discolouring. Remove the chokes and rub the insides with more salt and lemon.

To prepare the stuffing, melt the fat in the pan and fry the onions for 2–3 minutes. Add the mince and fry for 2–3 minutes until the meat soaks up its juices. Add the tomatoes and fry for a further 2 minutes. Season with salt and pepper, cover the pan and set aside.

Blend the flour to a paste with a little of the stock. Melt the butter in a pan, add the stock, lemon juice and flour paste. Bring to the boil, quickly rinse the artichokes and place them upside down in the pan. Put a sheet of greaseproof paper between the pan and the lid. Bring back to the boil, then simmer for 20 minutes.

Grease an oven dish. Remove the artichokes from the liquid and arrange them in the dish. Stuff each one, and place a slice of tomato on top. Pour in enough of the artichoke cooking liquid so that it comes half way up the artichokes. Cover the dish and cook in a preheated oven at 200°C/400°F/gas mark 6 for 35–40 minutes. Serve hot.

◊ KIYMALI LAHANA KAPAMASI ◊

CABBAGE LAYERED WITH MINCED MEAT

Kapama means "covered over"; in this case the minced meat is covered with layers of cabbage. The same ingredients can also be prepared by stuffing a whole cabbage with the meat, as in kapama of cabbage in olive oil (p.113).

TO SERVE 6
1 large white cabbage (1kg/2lb)
FOR THE FILLING
25g/1oz cooking fat or butter
25g/1oz pine nuts

200g/7oz onions, peeled and finely chopped
250g/8oz lamb, minced
1tsp tomato purée
½tsp red pepper
salt to taste
20g/¾oz parsley, chopped
25g/1oz currants

To prepare the filling soak the currants in water for 30 minutes.

Melt the fat in a pan, add the pine nuts and fry for 1 minute. Add the onions and fry for 4–5 minutes until golden. Add the mince and fry for 5–10 minutes, stirring occasionally until the meat absorbs its own juices. Add the tomato purée and stir for 1 minute. Sprinkle on the pepper and salt. Add the parsley with the currants, stir for 1 minute and remove from the heat.

Remove the coarse cabbage leaves. Cut down the middle into two halves, remove the stem and wash. Bring a large pan of salted water to the boil and add the cabbage. Cover and return to the boil, then transfer the cabbage to a strainer. Allow the leaves to cool, separate them and remove the stems.

Divide the cabbage leaves into three and the mince into two. Layer them in a flame-proof pan, ending with a layer of cabbage. Pour in 150ml/¼ pint water from the side, cover and cook for 25–30 minutes on low heat until the cabbage is tender, then under the grill for 10 minutes, until the top layer of leaves turns golden.

Cut across the dish with a sharp knife to make either square or diamond-shaped portions and serve in the pan.

◊ KABAK BASTISI ◊

COURGETTE RAGOUT

TO SERVE 4
500g/1lb courgettes
250g/8oz lamb, cubed
100g/3½oz onions, finely chopped
25g/1oz cooking fat or butter
25g/1oz tomato purée
100g/3½oz tomatoes, peeled, deseeded and chopped
25g/1oz mint sprigs
½tsp red pepper
½tsp caster sugar
2tbsp lemon juice or verjuice (p.173)
400ml/14fl oz hot stock
salt to taste

ACCOMPANIMENT
vermicelli pilaf (p.119) with crumbled cheese

Trim the courgettes and peel thinly in alternate strips. Cut into thick matchsticks.

Put the meat in a heavy pan and cover. Let it absorb its own juices on low heat, then add the onions and fat. Fry, uncovered, stirring occasionally for 4–5 minutes until the onions turn golden, add the tomato purée and stir for a further 1 minute.

Put the courgettes on top of the meat, then the tomatoes. Add the other ingredients, cover and cook for 30–40 minutes until the meat is tender.

Remove the mint and serve hot.

◊ BAMYA BASTISI ◊

OKRA RAGOUT

Bastı – vegetable ragout – can be made with a small amount of meat added, as for the okra and courgette ragouts featured here. Generally ragouts with fruit are cooked with rice but without meat.

TO SERVE 4
500g/1lb okra
50ml/2fl oz vinegar
2tbsp salt
250g/8oz lamb, cubed
50g/2oz cooking fat or melted sheep's tail fat
150g/5oz onions, finely chopped
200g/7oz tomatoes
400ml/14fl oz stock
50ml/2fl oz lemon juice or verjuice (p.173) or ½tsp lemon salt (p.173)
1tsp red pepper
1tsp salt or to taste
ACCOMPANIMENT
rice pilaf (p.119)

Trim the tops of the okra, pour vinegar over them, and sprinkle with salt; mix thoroughly with both hands, and leave for 30 minutes. This treatment "bleaches" the okra and prevents them from losing their texture.

Put the meat in a heavy pan, cover and place on the heat. When it absorbs its own juices and begins to sizzle, add the fat and onions and fry, uncovered, for 4–5 minutes, stirring occasionally, until the onions soften.

Peel all the tomatoes, cut one in half and remove the seeds; deseed and chop the rest. Put the halved tomato in the middle of a small pan. Wash the okra in plenty of water, arrange about half of them in a layer around the tomato with tops pointing inwards. Spread the meat on top, then arrange the remaining okra on top in the same fashion.

Fry the remaining tomatoes for 2 minutes in the pan in which the meat was fried. Add the meat stock. Bring to the boil and pour over the okra. Add the lemon juice, red pepper and salt, cover the pan and cook for 40–50 minutes on very low heat until the okra and meat are tender.

Pour off the liquid carefully and reserve. Put a serving dish over the pan, then invert it to turn out the okra. Pour the liquid over the dish and serve hot, with rice pilaf.

◊ PATATES SILKMESI ◊
POTATOES SILKME FASHION

Silkmeler are dishes prepared with small amounts of cubed or minced meat as in the recipe below. "Silkme" means shaken, and the pan is shaken from time to time during cooking so that nothing sticks. In this dish crushed cloves of garlic are sometimes added to the pan with the meat and potatoes.

TO SERVE 4
250g/8oz lamb, cubed
500ml/17fl oz water
150g/5oz cooking fat or sunflower oil for deep-frying
500g/1lb potatoes, peeled and thinly sliced
100g/3½oz onions, finely sliced
400g/14oz tomatoes, peeled, deseeded and chopped
50ml/2fl oz water
½tsp salt or to taste
½tsp ground cumin
1tsp red pepper
¼tsp ground black pepper

ACCOMPANIMENT
ayran (p.168)

Simmer the meat in the water for about 1 hour until tender, then drain. Heat the fat or oil and fry the potatoes for 5 minutes until golden. Transfer them to a colander, fry the meat in the fat used for the potatoes for 2 minutes and drain.

Leave 1tbsp of fat in the frying pan, add the onions and fry for 3 minutes. Add the tomatoes, stir-fry for 2 minutes, add the water and bring to the boil, add the salt, cumin, red and black pepper.

Put the potatoes and meat in a shallow pan with handles on both sides. Spread the onion mixture on top, cover the pan and cook for 10 minutes on very low heat, shaking the pan from time to time. The dish is ready when all the water has been absorbed and only the fat remains.

Serve hot with ayran.

◊ GÜVEÇTE YAZ TÜRLÜSÜ ◊
SUMMER STEW

TO SERVE 6	
6 small pieces of scrag end or middle neck of mutton	150g/5oz artichokes
	150g/5oz courgettes
100g/3½oz onions, sliced	150g/5oz aubergines
25g/1oz cooking fat or butter	salt to taste
25g/1oz tomato purée	50g/2oz green beans
1tsp red pepper	250g/8oz tomatoes
	25g/1oz green peppers
1L/1¾ pints stock	50g/2oz broad beans

Prepare the meat in the same way as for Winter Stew (below) and cook for 1 hour.

Prepare the artichokes as described on p.88, and divide into quarters. Peel the courgettes, cut lengthways into four and crossways into five. Peel the aubergines in alternate strips, cut the same way as the marrow and leave for 30 minutes sprinkled with salt. Cut the green beans in half or in three, depending on their size. Peel the tomatoes, slice into rings and deseed. Cut the peppers into two or three pieces.

Add all the vegetables to the meat in the pan, tomatoes and peppers last. Cover and cook for 30–40 minutes until the vegetables are tender.

Serve hot in the casserole.

◊ GÜVEÇTE KIŞ TÜRLÜSÜ ◊
WINTER STEW

Y ou can prepare this dish with seasonal vegetables, be it summer or winter. Türlü can also be cooked in small single-helping earthenware pots.

TO SERVE 6
6 small pieces of scrag end or middle neck of lamb
100g/3½oz onions, sliced
25g/1oz cooking fat or butter
25g/1oz tomato purée
1tsp red pepper
1L/1¾ pints stock
100g/3½oz celeriac
100g/3½oz carrots
100g/3½oz leeks
100g/3½oz turnips
100g/3½oz potatoes
100g/3½oz peas
salt to taste
ACCOMPANIMENT
bulgur or firik pilaf (p.119)
ayran (p.168)

Put the meat in a casserole on low heat and cover. When the meat absorbs its juices and begins to sizzle, add the onions and fat and fry for 3–4 minutes until the onions become golden. Add the tomato purée and stir for 1 minute. Sprinkle on the red pepper, add the stock and simmer for about 1 hour.

Cut the vegetables into thick slices. Put all the vegetables except the peas on the meat with the potatoes on top, and cook for a further 25–30 minutes until tender. Add the peas, sprinkle with salt if necessary, and cook for a further 10 minutes.

Serve hot in the casserole with a pilaf and ayran.

NOTE: This dish can also be cooked in the oven until the surface browns.

◊ PILIÇLI BAMYA GÜVECI ◊

CASSEROLE OF OKRA WITH CHICKEN

TO SERVE 4
4 small chicken breasts
500g/1lb okra
50g/2oz cooking fat or butter
200g/7oz onions, chopped
300g/10oz tomatoes, peeled, deseeded and chopped
25g/1 oz green pepper, chopped
25ml/1 fl oz lemon juice
½tsp salt or to taste
ACCOMPANIMENT
rice pilaf (p.119)

Prepare the okra and soak for 30 minutes as described on p.91.

Melt the fat in a pan, add the chicken breasts and fry on both sides for 5 minutes. Add the onions and fry for 3–4 minutes. Pour on 200ml/⅓ pint boiling water, cook for 15 minutes and transfer to an iron casserole.

Wash the okra thoroughly and add to the casserole with the other ingredients and 400ml/⅔ pint boiling water. Place a sheet of greaseproof paper between casserole and lid. Bring to the boil, reduce heat and cook for 30–40 minutes, or longer if necessary, until the okra are tender.

Serve in the casserole with rice pilaf.

◊ ALI NAZIK ◊

AUBERGINE PURÉE WITH
YOGHURT SAUCE AND MINCED MEAT

TO SERVE 6
500g/1lb aubergines
1 quantity yoghurt and garlic sauce (p.172)
salt to taste
25g/1oz cooking fat or butter
50g/2oz onions, finely chopped
125g/4oz minced lamb
1tbsp finely chopped green peppers
50g/2oz tomatoes, peeled, deseeded and chopped or 1tsp tomato purée
¼tsp ground black pepper
¼tsp red pepper
¼tsp dried thyme

Prepare and cook the aubergines as specified in the recipe for hünkar beğendi (p.64), purée and mix with half the quantity of yoghurt and garlic sauce. Sprinkle with salt if necessary.

Heat the fat in a pan and fry the onions for 3–4 minutes until golden. Add the mince and peppers and fry for 7–8 minutes, stirring, until the meat absorbs its own juices. Add the tomatoes and cook for 3–4 minutes until they soak up their juices, or add the tomato purée. Stir in the seasoning.

Spread the aubergine purée in a heated serving dish, and spread the remainder of the yoghurt sauce on top. Spread the mince over it. Serve straight away.

◊ ETLI KURU FASULYE ◊

HARICOT BEANS WITH MEAT

Haricot beans are the main ingredient of one of the most popular winter dishes in Turkey.

TO SERVE 6
500g/1lb haricot beans, soaked overnight
1 onion
300g/10oz shoulder of lamb
50g/2oz cooking fat
250g/8oz onions, finely chopped
25g/1oz tomato purée
1L/1¾ pints stock (p.33)
1tsp coarsely ground red pepper
salt to taste
ACCOMPANIMENTS
rice pilaf (p.119), ayran (p.168)
crushed onions (see below)

Drain the beans and put them in a pan with 1.5L/2½ pints cold water and the onion and bring to the boil. Remove from the heat and leave to stand.

Cut the meat into 6 pieces and sear in a dry pan for 10–15 minutes, stirring occasionally, until the juices are absorbed. Add the fat and onions. Stir for 4 minutes until the onions are golden. Add the tomato purée and stir for 1 minute. Pour on the stock, stir in the red pepper and cook on medium heat for 30–40 minutes.

Strain the beans and discard the onion. Add the beans to the pan and continue to cook for 20–30 minutes on medium heat until the beans are tender. Add salt to taste. If the beans are still hard after absorbing all the liquid, add more stock or water and continue cooking.

Place in a serving dish and serve hot with rice pilaf, ayran and onions, crushed with a wooden mallet.

◊ KIYMALI MERCIMEK ◊

GREEN LENTILS WITH MINCED MEAT

TO SERVE 2–3
150g/5oz green lentils, soaked for 3–4 hours
75g/3oz minced lamb
25g/1oz cooking fat or butter
100g/3½oz onions, finely chopped
1tsp tomato purée
1tsp salt
¼tsp ground black pepper
1L/1¾ pints stock
¼tsp chilli flakes

Put the lentils in a pan with 1L/1¾ pints fresh water. Boil for 10 minutes, remove from the heat and strain. Put the mince in a pan and dry-fry for 2 minutes, stirring. Add the fat and onions. Fry for 8–10 minutes until the onions are golden. Stir in the tomato purée, season, pour on the stock, sprinkle on the chilli flakes and cover. Once it boils, add the lentils and cook for 30–40 minutes until they are tender. Serve hot with potato salad (p.116).

◊ PATLICAN MUSAKKASI ◊

MOUSSAKA OF AUBERGINES

Musakkalar, fried vegetable dishes with minced meat, are made with potatoes or courgettes as well as the aubergines used in this recipe.

TO SERVE 4
500g/1lb aubergines
salt to taste
250g/8oz cooking fat or sunflower oil for deep frying
125g/4oz lean minced meat
150g/5oz onions, finely chopped
75g/3oz green peppers
250g/8oz tomatoes
1/2tsp ground black pepper
1/2tsp red pepper
300ml/1/2 pint stock

Score the skin of the aubergines at 2.5cm/ 1 inch intervals. Slice lengthways 1.25cm/ 1/2 inch thick, sprinkle with salt and leave for 30 minutes. Press gently to extract the bitter juices, wash, drain and dry.

Melt the fat and partly fry the aubergines for 2–3 minutes. Strain and set aside. Put the mince in another pan with the onions, and fry for 3–4 minutes, stirring occasionally, until the onions turn golden. Chop half the peppers finely and fry for 2–3 minutes. Peel, deseed and chop all but one of the tomatoes, add to the pan and fry for another 4–5 minutes until the tomatoes absorb their juices. Sprinkle with salt, black and red pepper.

In a casserole make alternate layers with the aubergines and minced meat, ending with the meat.

Slice the remaining tomato and pepper and place them on the top layer of mince. Add the hot stock, cover and bring to the boil, then cover and simmer gently for 20–30 minutes. If you cook the moussaka in the oven, cook for 20 minutes with the lid on and 5 minutes uncovered.

Serve hot.

FRUIT WITH MEAT

In Turkish cuisine, fruit is often combined with meat to extend the range of flavours in the main course.

In central Anatolia and in Konya in particular a wide range of unusual fruit dishes is commonplace in daily menus. This is due to the huge variety of local fruit and to the ingenuity of Anatolian women, keen to outshine each other in producing exotic dishes from their kitchen gardens and small orchards.

Fruit dishes can be sweetened with sugar or pekmez – grape syrup (p.173). Konya pekmez, which has a faintly bitter taste, contributes a distinctive flavour, but other syrups may be used instead.

◊ **AYVA YAHNISI** ◊

S T E W E D   Q U I N C E S

TO SERVE 6	50g/2oz butter or cooking fat
600g/1¼lb double or single loin chops	small piece cinnamon
400g/14oz quinces	50g/2oz caster sugar
50g/2oz onions, grated	A C C O M P A N I M E N T
½tsp salt	*iç pilav – prepared without yufka* (p.125)

Cook the meat as for Wedding Stew (p.77) and strain, reserving the liquid. Rub with grated onions and salt. Heat the butter and fry both sides of the meat for 4 minutes, then return the meat to the liquid and reserve the butter. Add the cinnamon to the meat, and cook for approximately 1½ hours until the meat is tender.

Cut the unpeeled quinces into quarters, core them and cut in two crossways, wash and dry. Stir-fry in the reserved butter for 1 minute. Add the quinces to the meat and cook for 10 minutes. Add the sugar, bring to the boil, reduce to very low heat and cook for 15–20 minutes or until the quinces are tender but still whole.

◊ AYVA DOLMASI ◊

CLAUDIA'S DELIGHT

When Claudia Roden ate quince dolmas in Konya, she showed her knowledge of local cooking by remarking: "The Imam loved aubergine dolmas and I love quince dolmas." For this reason I am naming this dish Claudia's Delight.

TO SERVE 6
6 small quinces
50g/2oz butter
150g/5oz caster sugar
FOR THE STUFFING
25g/1oz currants
25g/1oz rice
salt
¼tsp ground cinnamon
200g/7oz fat shoulder or scrag end of neck of lamb, minced
FOR THE GARNISH
6 quince leaves

To prepare the stuffing, soak the currants in warm water for 30 minutes, wash and drain. Soak the rice in 200ml/7fl oz warm water with 1tsp salt, and leave until cool. Wash and drain. Put it in a pan with 200ml/7fl oz boiling water and boil for 5 minutes. Dry-fry the minced meat on medium heat for 2–3 minutes to sear. Knead together the meat, rice and currants, and sprinkle with salt and cinnamon.

To prepare the dolmas, wash the unpeeled quinces, core, hollow out with a scoop or teaspoon and fill with the stuffing. Place the quinces in a shallow pan. Divide the butter into 6 pieces and place one on each quince. Sprinkle on the sugar. Add 200ml/6fl oz hot water, cover the pan, and put in a preheated oven at 200°C/400°F/gas mark 6. Cook for 40–50 minutes, until the quinces are tender.

Put them in a heated serving dish and top each one with a quince leaf to serve.

◊ ERIK DOLMASI ◊

DOLMAS OF DRIED GREENGAGES

This dolma recipe is from Konya. You can also prepare dried greengages in yahni fashion (p.98) – as a stew. Prunes can be used instead of dried greengages.

TO SERVE 4
125g/4oz dried greengages
25g/1oz butter
150g/5oz caster sugar
FOR THE STUFFING
½ quantity stuffing for quince dolmas but without the currants (p.99)

Prepare the stuffing. Wash the dried greengages and put them in a pan with 1 L/ 1¾ pints cold water. Bring to the boil and simmer for about 10 minutes until they are ready to open in the middle.

Drain and reserve the cooking water. Fill the greengages with the stuffing, put them in a shallow pan with small pieces of butter in between, pour on 200ml/7fl oz reserved cooking liquor and cover the pan. Bring to the boil, sprinkle with the sugar and cover again. Cook on a very low heat for 40 minutes until the greengages and rice are tender.

Leave for 10 minutes, then serve hot in the pan.

◊ ELMA DIZMESI ◊

APPLES DIZME FASHION

This dish of apples and meat patties from southeastern Anatolia can also be prepared with pekmez – grape syrup (p.173) – instead of sugar. Dizme means "lined up" and refers to the way the apples and köfte are arranged in the pan.

TO SERVE 6
500g/1lb hard cooking apples
500g/1lb fat shoulder of lamb, minced twice
¼tsp crushed cloves
½tsp salt
200ml/7fl oz boiling water
25g/1oz butter
150g/5oz caster sugar

Core the apples and slice in rings 1.25cm/ ½inch thick. If the apples are large, cut them in half and then slice them.

Knead the mince well with the cloves and salt and make köfte the same size as the apple slices. Stand them upright in alternate rows in a shallow pan, just large enough to hold them. Add the water, dot with pieces of butter and cover the pan. Bring to the boil, sprinkle the sugar over everything and cook on very low heat for about 30 minutes until the apples and köfte are tender.

◊ KESTANELI YAHNI ◊
STEWED CHESTNUTS WITH LAMB

This unusual recipe comes from Istanbul.

TO SERVE 6
600g/1¼lb single or double loin lamb chops
300g/10oz chestnuts
50g/2oz cooking fat
100g/3½oz onions, chopped
½tsp salt
small piece cinnamon
25g/1oz caster or granulated sugar

Prepare the meat as for Wedding Stew (p.77), reserving the fat.

Slit the skin of each chestnut, and grill to loosen the skin. Shell the nuts and fry for 2 minutes in the fat used to fry the meat, stirring frequently.

Add the chestnuts to the meat, reduce the heat to very low and cook for 10 minutes. Add the sugar and cook for a further 10 minutes or until the chestnuts are tender.

Serve hot.

◊ KAYISILI YAHNI ◊
STEWED APRICOTS WITH LAMB

This version of stewed apricots is yet another speciality of Konya. It acquires a particularly delicious flavour when made with the sour apricots grown there. It can be served on slices of baked stale bread, as a tırıt (p.128).

TO SERVE 4
250G/8oz fat scrag end of neck of lamb on the bone
1L/1¾ pints water
250g/8oz dried sour apricots (avoid choice sweet fruit)
25–50g/1–2oz butter
1tsp salt
300g/10oz caster sugar (or to taste)
ACCOMPANIMENT
slices of stale bread, baked in the oven until crisp

Put the meat in a pan, add the water and bring to the boil. Skim, then cover and simmer for 1 hour until the meat is cooked. Remove the meat from the bone, and return to the cooking liquor.

Pick over and wash the apricots, add them to the meat, and cover the pan. Bring to the boil, add the butter and salt and reduce the heat to very low. Cook for 10 minutes until the apricots are tender. Add the sugar and cook for another 20–25 minutes.

Arrange the baked bread on a serving dish, top with the meat and apricots, and serve hot.

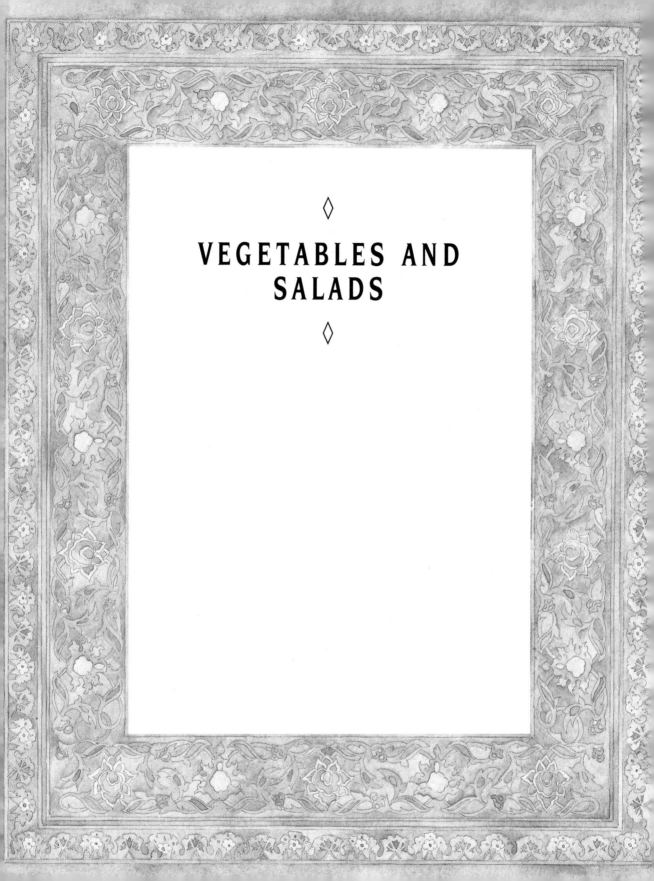

◊

VEGETABLES AND SALADS

◊

◊ YALANCI DOLMA ◊

VEGETABLE DOLMAS

These dolmas are called "yalancı" – imitations – because they contain no meat, the main ingredient in the stuffing of "true" dolmas.

Yalancı dolmas are served mainly on picnics, with cold buffets and as mezes, but also as a light dish for lunch.

FOR THE STUFFING
150g/5oz rice
25g/1oz currants
200ml/7fl oz olive oil
25g/1 oz pine nuts
450g/15oz onions, finely chopped
25g/1oz tomato purée
¹⁄₄tsp ground black pepper
¹⁄₄tsp ground allspice
¹⁄₄tsp ground cinnamon
¹⁄₄tsp red pepper
¹⁄₈tsp ground cloves
1tbsp caster sugar   salt
a few sprigs each of parsley, dill and mint, chopped

Soak the rice in salted warm water until the water is cold. Soak the currants in plain warm water for 1 hour.

Pour the olive oil into a pan. Fry the pine nuts for 2 minutes, then add the onions and fry for 10–15 minutes until golden. Drain the rice and fry for 3 minutes. Stir in the tomato purée, then add the spices, sugar and a pinch of salt. Pour on enough boiling water just to cover. Cover the pan and cook for 3 minutes on medium heat, then on low heat for 10–15 minutes. The stuffing should be only partly cooked. Stir in the herbs, cover the pan and leave for 10 minutes. Use for dolmas and sarmas.

◊ YALANCI ASMA YAPRAĞI ◊ SARMASI

SARMA OF VINE LEAVES

TO SERVE 8–10
1 quantity yalancı dolma stuffing (above)
200g/7oz vine leaves, fresh or preserved
200ml/7fl oz water
25ml/1fl oz lemon juice
salt to taste
FOR THE GARNISH
lemon slices

Prepare the stuffing and the vine leaves (p.85). Place 2–3 leaves in the bottom of a heavy pan, stuff all but 2 or 3 of the remaining leaves and roll them up like cigarettes. (Meat-filled vine leaves should be short and fat, yalancı sarmas long and thin.) Arrange them in the pan and cover with the remaining leaves. Add water and lemon juice, salt to taste and cover the sarmas with a plate to stop them unrolling. Put on the lid and bring to the boil, lower the heat and cook for 1 hour. Leave to cool in the pan, garnish with lemon slices. Serve cold.

◊ YALANCI BIBER DOLMASI ◊
VEGETABLE - STUFFED PEPPERS

TO SERVE 6
1 quantity yalancı dolma stuffing (p.103)
500g/1lb small peppers suitable for stuffing
300ml/7fl oz water
25ml/1fl oz lemon juice
salt to taste
FOR THE GARNISH
lemon slices
ACCOMPANIMENT
watermelon

Prepare the stuffing and the peppers as described on p.85. Stuff the peppers and arrange them in a pan. Pour on the water and lemon juice, sprinkle with salt and cover the pan. Bring to the boil, reduce the heat to very low and simmer for 45 minutes. Leave to cool in the pan.

Place the peppers on a serving dish, garnish with lemon slices around the edges and serve cold with watermelon.

◊ YALANCI ENGINAR DOLMASI ◊
ARTICHOKES STUFFED WITH BROAD BEANS

TO SERVE 6
6 large artichokes
1 lemon
50ml/2fl oz olive oil
1tbsp caster sugar
1tbsp flour
250ml/7fl oz water
25ml/1fl oz lemon juice
FOR THE STUFFING
50ml/2fl oz olive oil
100g/3½oz onions, finely chopped
100g/3½oz broad beans, podded and skins removed
½tsp salt
50g/2oz rice
200ml/7fl oz boiling water
a few sprigs dill, chopped
FOR THE GARNISH
lemon slices
1tbsp chopped dill

To prepare the stuffing, heat the oil and fry the onions for 2–3 minutes. Chop the broad beans finely and add with the salt. Wash and drain the rice and add. Fry the mixture for another 5 minutes. Add the water, cover the pan and cook for 15 minutes on very low heat. Stir in the dill. Remove from the heat, and leave in the covered pan.

Prepare the artichokes as described on p.88. Wash, rub with lemon again, stuff and arrange in a casserole, pour the olive oil around the edge, sprinkle with sugar.

Whisk the flour, water and lemon juice together in a pan and bring to the boil. Pour into the casserole almost up to the top of the artichokes. Place 2 sheets of greaseproof paper between the casserole and the lid, cover and cook in the oven at 200°C/400°F/gas mark 6 for 40–50 minutes, or until the artichokes are tender. Allow the artichokes to cool in the pan, then lift out carefully, transfer to a serving dish, garnish with lemon slices and dill and serve cold.

◊ MÜCVER ◊
C O U R G E T T E   P A T T I E S

Patties are an ideal food for cold buffets and picnics.

TO SERVE 6–8.
500g/1lb courgettes
100g/3½oz onions
200ml/7fl oz olive oil
100g/3½oz soft white cheese, grated or crumbled
100g/3½oz flour
4 eggs
20g/¾oz chopped dill
1tsp salt (less if cheese is salty)
½tsp ground black pepper

Wash and grate the courgettes and squeeze out the juices by pressing firmly in your hands or in a muslin cloth. Prepare the onions in the same way.

Heat 1tbsp olive oil, add the onion and courgette and fry for 1 minute, stirring. Transfer to a bowl and allow to cool.

Mix in the cheese, flour and egg. Add the dill, sprinkle with salt and pepper, and mix thoroughly.

Heat the remaining oil. Put spoonfuls of the mixture into the pan, spaced well apart. Fry for 2 minutes, then turn and fry the other side for 3 minutes. Transfer to absorbent paper. Serve hot or cold.

◊ KARIŞIK YAZ TAVASI ◊
F R I E D   S U M M E R   V E G E T A B L E S

TO SERVE 6
200g/7oz aubergine
1tbsp salt
200g/7oz marrow or courgettes
200g/7oz thin green peppers
olive oil or sunflower oil   *for deep frying*
1 quantity yoghurt and garlic sauce (p.172)
1 quantity tomato sauce (p.124)

Prepare the yoghurt and garlic sauce and tomato purée and keep at room temperature.

Peel the aubergine and slice crossways. Sprinkle with salt, leave for 30 minutes, squeeze to get rid of any bitter juices, wash and dry. Peel the marrow or courgettes thinly, and slice like the aubergine, wash and dry. Wash the peppers with stems on, dry.

Heat the oil and briefly deep-fry first the aubergine, then the marrow or courgettes, followed by the peppers. When golden, transfer in turn to absorbent paper.

Place the vegetables on a heated serving dish. As you serve, pour over each helping plenty of yoghurt and garlic sauce and top it with tomato sauce.

NOTE: If the sauces are poured over the dish too long before being eaten, the vegetables will lose their crispness.

◊ IMAM BAYILDI ◊

IMAM'S DELIGHT

The name of this dish of stuffed aubergines in olive oil – Imam Bayıldı – has been mistranslated in a number of books as "The Imam Fainted", but no Turk would faint at a dish made from two of our basic ingredients.

There are many stories told about Imam Bayıldı, and this one comes from an elderly lady in Konya and has to do with the Turkish woman's characteristic keenness to be a good hostess.

In the old days in Anatolia it was customary for the local imam to be invited for a meal by members of his congregation. To have the imam as a guest for a meal was considered an honour for the household.

One day a shopkeeper on his way home heard the call for evening prayers and went into the mosque. After prayers – so the story goes – he invited the priest for a meal, without a thought as to the position at home, and they went to his house. That day his wife had been busy doing the washing and had not prepared a meal. She was naturally very upset, and hurriedly concocted a meal of stuffed aubergines in olive oil and served it. While she waited anxiously in the kitchen, her husband came in smiling and said: "Don't worry my dear, the imam was delighted by your dish!"

TO SERVE 4
4 medium aubergines
salt
olive oil for frying
1 green pepper, sliced into rings
FOR THE STUFFING
400g/14oz onions, finely sliced

7 cloves of garlic, chopped
150g/5oz tomatoes, peeled and finely sliced
1tsp tomato purée
½tsp salt
1tsp caster sugar
3 sprigs parsley, chopped

Remove the stalks from the aubergines and peel the skin either entirely or in strips at 2.5cm/1 inch intervals. Cut in half lengthways, rub with salt, and leave for 20 minutes. Soak in water for 5 minutes, then drain. Fry in boiling hot oil for 5 minutes. Transfer the aubergines to a shallow flame-proof casserole that will just hold them in a single layer.

Pour a further 50ml/2fl oz oil into the pan. Add the onions and garlic and fry for 5 minutes. Add the tomatoes and tomato purée and fry for 3 minutes. Add 150ml/¼ pint of water, the salt and sugar and cook for 10 minutes on low heat. Strain and reserve the liquid. Add the parsley.

Fill the aubergines with the onion mixture, and top each one with a sliced pepper ring. Add the strained cooking liquid and cook for 40–50 minutes on a very low heat. Allow to cool and serve the dish cold in the cooking pan.

◊ ZEYTINYAĞLI BARBUNYA ◊ FASULYESI

BORLOTTI BEANS IN OLIVE OIL

TO SERVE 4
200g/7oz borlotti beans
1 small whole onion
50ml/2fl oz olive oil
100g/3½oz onions, chopped
100g/3½oz carrots
1tsp tomato purée
150g/5oz tomatoes, peeled and diced
800ml/1 pint 7fl oz stock or water
1tsp caster sugar
salt to taste
FOR THE GARNISH
1tbsp chopped parsley
ACCOMPANIMENT
rice pilaf (p.119)

Soak the beans in hot water for 8 hours. Drain and wash them and put in a pan with 1L/1¾ pints fresh water and the small onion; cover the pan. Bring to the boil, cook for 1 hour, remove the onion and drain.

Put the olive oil in a pan, add the chopped onions and fry for 4–5 minutes. Peel the carrots and chop to the same size as the beans, add and fry for a further 2 minutes. Add the tomato purée and stir for 1 minute, then the tomatoes and stir for 3–4 minutes. Add the stock or water and sugar; cover the pan. Bring to the boil and add the beans, cover and cook for 40 minutes on low heat until the beans are tender. Season with salt and cook for a further 5 minutes, remove from the heat and allow to cool in the pan. Sprinkle on chopped parsley and serve cold with rice pilaf.

◊ ZEYTINYAĞLI EKŞILI PIRASA ◊
SOUR LEEKS IN OLIVE OIL

TO SERVE 4
500g/1lb leeks, trimmed and cut into matchsticks
150g/5oz onions, finely sliced
50ml/2fl oz olive oil
25g/1 oz tomato purée
4 cloves of garlic, finely chopped
a few sprigs of parsley, chopped
1tsp salt
1tsp caster sugar
600ml/1 pint stock or water
25ml/1fl oz lemon juice

Sweat the leeks in a little water for 2–3 minutes, shaking the pan occasionally. Strain and transfer to a heatproof casserole. Fry the onions in the olive oil for 4–5 minutes. Add the tomato purée and stir for 1 minute. Add the garlic and parsley, sprinkle with salt and sugar, stir and remove from the heat.

Spread the onion mixture over the leeks, add the stock and cover the casserole. Bring to the boil, add the lemon juice, then reduce to very low heat and cook until the leeks are tender.

As soon as you remove the pan from the heat, place under a preheated grill and brown for 10 minutes.

Allow to cool in the pan and serve cold.

◊ ZEYTINYAĞLI TAZE FASULYE ◊
GREEN BEANS IN OLIVE OIL

TO SERVE 4
500g/1lb runner beans, cut into 2.5cm/1 inch lengths
150g/5oz onions, sliced
25g/1 oz thin green peppers, split in half
1tsp salt
1tsp tomato purée
50ml/2fl oz olive oil
100g/3½oz tomatoes, peeled and finely chopped
200ml/7fl oz water
1tsp caster sugar

Mix together the beans, onions, peppers, salt and tomato purée. Heat the oil in a pan, add the vegetables, cover and fry them lightly for 5 minutes, shaking the pan occasionally. Add the tomatoes, water and sugar and cook until the beans are tender. Leave to cool in the pan. Transfer to a serving dish and serve cold.

◊ ZEYTINYAĞLI KEREVIZ ◊

CELERIAC IN OLIVE OIL

TO SERVE 4
500g/1lb celeriac
salt
25ml/1fl oz lemon juice
100g/3½oz carrots
100g/3½oz potatoes
100ml/3½fl oz olive oil
200g/7oz onions, chopped
500ml/17fl oz stock
1tsp caster sugar
FOR THE GARNISH
a few sprigs parsley, chopped
50g/2oz boiled fresh peas

Peel the celeriac, cut in half, remove any hard core, wash and parboil for 5 minutes in water to which you have added salt and a squeeze of lemon juice. Drain and chop.

Peel the carrots, cut lengthways into quarters and chop into 5–6cm/2–2½ inch lengths. Peel the potatoes and cut up the same size as the carrots.

Place the oil, onions and carrots in a pan and fry for 4–5 minutes on medium heat, stirring. Add the parboiled celeriac, the stock, a pinch of salt and the sugar. Bring to the boil, then reduce to low heat and add the potatoes after 10 minutes. Cook for a further 20 minutes until the vegetables are really tender. Allow to cool in the pan. Pile the vegetables on top of the celeriac on a serving dish. Serve cold, garnished with parsley and peas.

NOTE: You can add raw rather than parboiled celeriac to the fried onions for a stronger flavour.

◊ ZEYTINYAĞLI HAVUÇ ◊

CARROTS IN OLIVE OIL

TO SERVE 6
100g/3½oz green lentils
50ml/2fl oz olive oil
150g/5oz onions, thinly sliced
1tbsp tomato purée
500g/1lb carrots, thinly sliced
1tsp salt
1tsp coarsely ground red pepper
FOR THE DRESSING
1 quantity yoghurt and garlic sauce (p.172)

Soak the lentils for a few hours, drain and put them in a pan with 500ml/17fl oz cold water. Bring to the boil and simmer for 10–20 minutes until tender; strain.

Heat the oil in a pan and fry the onions for 5–6 minutes, stirring, until golden. Add the tomato purée and stir for 1 minute.

Put the carrots in a pan, followed by the onion mixture, then the lentils. Add the salt and red pepper, and pour on 500ml/ 17fl oz hot water.

Bring to the boil and simmer for 30 minutes or longer until the carrots are really tender and the water has been absorbed. Leave to cool in the pan.

Transfer to a serving dish and spread with yoghurt and garlic sauce, or serve the sauce separately.

◊ NEVIN'IN ŞAŞTIM AŞI ◊

NEVIN'S SURPRISE DISH

Şaştım aşı is a flexible recipe for a summer dish that is particularly common in Sivas and Kayseri in central Anatolia.

In the past it was not the done thing for a lady to go shopping in the market or to the grocer's. Consequently, it required a great deal of skill for the lady of the house to remain unflustered if an unexpected guest arrived, and be able to devise a meal with whatever foods were in the house. Of course, in those days larders were stocked with ample quantities of all kinds of food and every house had a kitchen garden providing vegetables and fruit. Any shortage of good food in such homes could only be attributed to a certain lack of talent on the part of the lady concerned.

Nowadays townhouses have scarcely any garden or kitchen garden or larder; refrigerators have taken over. However, in Anatolia the tradition of preparing şaştım aşı still persists.

My dear reader, whoever you might be, whichever country you may come from; if some day you find yourself in Konya, please do not hesitate to call on me. As befits an Anatolian, there will always be a şaştım aşı which I can prepare for you in my kitchen with the greatest of pleasure throughout the four seasons.

Are you wondering what would follow? No doubt there would be Turkish coffee prepared over a charcoal brazier accompanied by lokum to complement the şaştım aşı.

You can find lokum on p.157.

TO SERVE 6
150g/5oz courgettes
150g/5oz aubergines
150g/5oz thin green peppers
250g/8oz ripe tomatoes
50g/2oz onions
50ml/2fl oz olive oil
1tsp tomato purée
100ml/3½fl oz water
1tsp salt
1tsp caster sugar
1 quantity of yoghurt and garlic sauce (p.172)
FOR THE GARNISH
1tsp haspir – safflower

Peel the courgettes thinly, cut into quarers lengthways and then cut across. Peel the aubergines in alternate strips and cut the same way as the courgettes, sprinkle with salt, leave for 20 minutes, then wash and drain. Top and tail the peppers, remove the seeds and chop into 3cm/1¼ inch lengths. Peel and deseed the tomatoes and chop roughly.

Chop the onions finely and fry in the oil for 2–3 minutes. Add the tomato purée and stir; add the courgettes, aubergines and peppers and stir-fry for 2–3 minutes until the vegetables change colour. Add the tomatoes, stir for 1 minute, then add the water. Sprinkle on the salt and sugar, cover the pan and cook for 15–20 minutes until the vegetables are tender and have absorbed the liquid.

Prepare the yoghurt and garlic sauce. When the vegetables are lukewarm, mix in half the yoghurt sauce, and transfer to a serving dish. Spread the remainder of the sauce over the dish, sprinkle with safflower and serve.

◊ MEYANELİ MANTAR YEMEĞİ ◊

MUSHROOMS IN SAUCE

TO SERVE 2
250g/8oz mushrooms, quartered
25g/1oz butter
50g/2oz onions, sliced
25g/1oz small green pepper, finely chopped
50g/2oz tomatoes, peeled and chopped
500ml/17fl oz hot water
1tsp salt
FOR THE SAUCE
1tbsp butter
1tbsp plain flour

Melt the butter and fry the onions until golden. Add the mushrooms, stir for 2 minutes, then the green pepper and stir for 1 minute. Add the tomatoes and stir for 3–4 minutes. Add the water and salt and cook for about 20 minutes until the mushrooms are very tender and there is a lot of juice.

While the vegetables are cooking, melt the butter for the sauce in another pan. Remove from the heat and mix in the flour. Return to the heat and stir until the flour turns golden. Remove the pan from the heat before it turns brown, and leave to cool.

When the mushrooms are ready, take a small amount of liquid from the pan and mix it with the roux to form a sauce. Stir it into the mushroom dish. Cook for a further 5 minutes, then serve.

◊ ISPANAK BORANISI ◊

SPINACH WITH YOGHURT SAUCE

Dishes of leafy green vegetables prepared with a yoghurt and garlic sauce and piping hot butter poured over them are known as borani.

TO SERVE 6
500g/1lb spinach, washed and sliced
50g/2oz cooking fat or butter
100g/3½oz onions, finely chopped
200ml/7fl oz water
½tsp salt or to taste
100g/3½oz rice, washed
1½ quantities of yoghurt with garlic sauce (p.172)
25g/1oz butter

Melt the fat and fry the onions for 3–4 minutes. Add the spinach, water and salt. Cover the pan. When it comes to the boil, reduce the heat to very low and add the rice. Cook for 15–20 minutes until the rice is tender. Remove the pan from the heat.

Prepare the yoghurt and garlic sauce and stir it into the pan. Turn the spinach out on to a serving dish, melt the butter, pour it over the spinach and serve hot.

◊ LAHANA KAPAMASI ◊

STUFFED CABBAGE

In this dish the cabbage is stuffed whole: it looks quite spectacular.

TO SERVE 6–8
1 large green cabbage
salt
50ml/2fl oz olive oil
FOR THE STUFFING
1 quantity yalancı dolma stuffing (p.103) without the mint and dill
FOR THE GARNISH
lemon slices
parsley sprigs

Remove the tough outer leaves of the cabbage, cut around the stalk and remove it. Discard the inner leaves to make a hollow sphere of 3–4 layers of the outer leaves. Wash the cabbage shell. Fill a large pan with water, add 1tsp salt, place the cabbage in it and leave to stand for 10 minutes. Drain.

Stuff the hollow cabbage and cover the top with a few of the discarded leaves. Place it in a deep pan. Add a pinch of salt, 200ml/7fl oz water and the olive oil, cover the pan, bring to the boil and cook gently for approximately 30 minutes until the cabbage is tender and the stuffing is cooked. Leave to cool in the pan.

Drain off the liquid, cover and turn the cabbage out on to the lid. Place a serving dish upside down on the cabbage and invert so it is the right way up again. Garnish with lemon slices and chopped parsley. Serve with extra lemon juice.

◊ TAHINLI TURP SALATASI ◊

RADISH AND TAHINA SALAD

This recipe is from Adana in southern Anatolia. It is a good accompaniment to içli köfte (p.70).

TO SERVE 4
250g/8oz white radish
salt
FOR THE DRESSING
1 clove garlic
4tbsp tahina
8tbsp Seville orange or grapefruit juice
FOR THE GARNISH
Seville orange or grapefruit slices
a few stoned olives, chopped

Peel the radish, grate, sprinkle with salt, leave for 3–4 minutes, then rub and squeeze out the juice. Arrange the orange or grapefruit slices round the rim of a serving dish and pile the radish in the middle.

Peel the garlic and pound with a pinch of salt. Add the tahina. Mix in the orange or grapefruit juice to combine. If necessary use a little more juice or water. Pour over the salad, garnish with the olives and serve.

◊ CACIK ◊

CUCUMBER SALAD WITH YOGHURT SAUCE

Cacık is one of the best-known dishes of Turkish cuisine.

TO SERVE 4
1 quantity yoghurt and garlic sauce (p.172)
200g/7oz cucumber
salt
1tbsp chopped dill
FOR THE GARNISH
1tbsp olive oil
¼tsp red pepper

Make the yoghurt and garlic sauce. Peel the cucumber, grate it, sprinkle with salt, leave for 1 hour, then squeeze out the juice. If you prefer your cacık crisp, cut the cucumber into thin slices and use it straight away. Mix it into the yoghurt with the chopped dill, transfer to a serving dish, pour the olive oil over gently, sprinkle with red pepper and serve.

◊ ÇOBAN ◊

TOMATO SALAD

The most popular Turkish salad; to be found everywhere.

TO SERVE 6
100g/3½oz onions, thinly sliced
½tsp salt
500g/1lb tomatoes, peeled, deseeded and chopped
100g/3½oz cucumber, peeled and chopped like the tomatoes
25g/1oz thin green peppers, deseeded and finely chopped
5–6 sprigs mint, chopped
a small bunch parsley, chopped
FOR THE DRESSING
25ml/1fl oz lemon juice or vinegar
25ml/1fl oz olive oil
salt to taste
FOR THE GARNISH
a few stoned olives

Sprinkle the onions with salt, leave for 3 minutes, rub with your fingers, rinse and squeeze out the juices in your hands or in a muslin cloth.

Put the onions on a serving dish, then the tomato, cucumber, peppers, mint and parsley in that order, with the olives on top. Whisk the lemon juice or vinegar with the olive oil and salt and pour over the salad when you are ready to serve it.

◊ BEYIN SALATASI ◊

B R A I N S   S A L A D

The 11th-century Classical Turkish Dictionary refers to the slaying of a sheep to celebrate the arrival of an honoured guest, and since the brain is the best part of the animal, this is served to the guest.

Brains salad would usually be served at a drinks supper.

TO SERVE 4
3 sheep's brains
1 small onion, quartered
1tbsp vinegar
1tsp salt
a small cos lettuce
7–8 stoned olives

FOR THE DRESSING
25ml/1fl oz lemon juice
25ml/1fl oz olive oil
salt to taste

Remove the membranes from the brains under running water. Put them in a pan with 1L/1¾ pints water, the onion, vinegar and salt. Bring to the boil, then cover and simmer for 15 minutes. Cool in the liquid, then remove the brains and slice lengthways into a serving dish in two rows.

Wash and dry the lettuce, shred it and put it around the brain. Garnish with olives.

Whisk the lemon juice, olive oil and salt, pour gently over the salad and serve.

◊ PATATES PIYAZI ◊

POTATO AND ONION SALAD

Potato and onion salad is very popular throughout Anatolia. In Bolu in north-western Anatolia, for example, it is served to guests as an entrée like kısır (p.39), before tea.

TO SERVE 4
250g/8oz potatoes
150g/5oz onions
salt
1tsp ground cumin
½tsp red pepper
½tsp ground black pepper
FOR THE GARNISH
6tbsp chopped parsley
2 hardboiled eggs, sliced lengthways
10–15 stoned olives

FOR THE DRESSING
25ml/1fl oz lemon juice
25ml/1fl oz olive oil

Boil the potatoes in their skins until barely cooked, drain and cool under cold running water. When cool, peel and grate into a bowl.

Slice the onions in rings, sprinkle with salt, leave for 3 minutes, rub, rinse, squeeze out the excess water and add the onions to the potatoes. Add a pinch of salt, the cumin, red and black pepper and mix. Arrange in the middle of a serving dish. Surround with most of the parsley, lay the sliced egg in a daisy pattern on top. Garnish with olives and the remaining parsley.

Whisk the lemon juice and olive oil in a bowl, pour gently over the salad and serve.

◊ MAŞ PIYAZI ◊

MUNG BEAN AND ONION SALAD

TO SERVE 4
150g/5oz mung beans
50g/2oz spring onions, finely chopped
50g/2oz chives, finely chopped
a few sprigs of parsley, chopped
1tsp chilli flakes
½tsp salt
2tbsp pomegranate seeds
FOR THE DRESSING
25ml/1fl oz pomegranate syrup (p.173) mixed with 50ml/2fl oz water or 50ml/2fl oz lemon juice

ACCOMPANIMENT
unleavened bread (yufka ekmeği, p.127)

Pick over and wash the mung beans and put them in a pan, add 1L/1¾ pints cold water and cover. Bring to the boil, turn down the heat and cook for 30 minutes. Drain and rinse the beans in cold water, then strain well. Mix in the onions, chives, parsley, chilli flakes and salt.

Put the salad in a dish and sprinkle with the pomegranate seeds. Mix the pomegranate syrup with water and pour over the salad. Serve with unleavened bread.

◊ FASULYE PIYAZI ◊
HARICOT BEAN AND ONION SALAD

This salad is served everywhere in Turkey. In southeastern Turkey, pitta stuffed with salads made with haricots or chickpeas or black-eyed beans and onion are sold by street vendors. In Gaziantep and Şanlı Urfa there are also special salad snack bars.

TO SERVE 4
250g/8oz dried haricot beans, soaked overnight
250g/8oz onions
1tsp salt
50g/2oz pickled cucumber
a small bunch parsley, chopped
FOR THE GARNISH
tomato slices
stoned olives
FOR THE DRESSING
50ml/2fl oz lemon juice
50ml/2fl oz olive oil
salt to taste

Boil the beans with 1 onion until the beans are tender. Cool in the liquid and drain.

Slice the remaining onions in fine rings, rub with salt, leave to rest for 3 minutes, then rub again, wash and squeeze out the juice. Chop the pickled cucumber the same size as the beans.

Mix the beans, onions and pickle together and arrange down the middle of a long serving dish. Surround with chopped parsley, and put sliced tomatoes at each end of the dish. Put pairs of olives at intervals on the beans.

Whisk the lemon juice, olive oil and salt, pour over the salad and serve.

NOTE: This salad can also be made with a purée of beans, with the other ingredients arranged on top.

◊ SOĞAN PIYAZI ◊
ONION SALAD

Onion salad invariably accompanies kebabs and köfte, be it at home, in restaurants or from a street vendor.

TO SERVE 6
500g/1lb onions
1tbsp salt
20g/¾oz parsley, finely chopped
1tsp sumac (p.173)

FOR THE GARNISH
4–5 stoned olives

Slice the onions finely in rings, sprinkle with the salt and leave for 4 minutes. Rub well with your fingers, rinse and squeeze out the excess water. Put the onions in a bowl and mix in half the parsley.

Arrange the onions on a serving dish, sprinkle with sumac, surround with the remaining parsley and olives and serve.

RICE AND GRAIN

◊ PILAVLAR ◊

PILAFS

Turkish cuisine has many varieties of pilaf. Rice, bulgur or wheat is the predominant ingredient in a plain pilaf and additional ingredients increase the variety.

In many parts of Anatolia it was not customary for young men to express openly to their parents their wish to get married. If one day, during the course of a meal, a young man stuck his spoon in the middle of the communal dish of pilaf and left the table, his family would understand from the gesture that he wished to get married, to leave the family and set up his own home. In popular speech the term "to throw rice" means to throw a wedding banquet.

WAYS OF COOKING PILAF

There are three ways of cooking pilaf:

1 Salma or free method: the basic ingredient is put into boiling stock and cooked until the stock is absorbed, then fat is heated to boiling point and poured over it.

2 Süzme or strained method: the basic ingredient is boiled in salted water, strained, and boiling fat is poured over it.

3 Kavurma or fried method: the basic ingredient is first fried and then cooked in stock until the stock is absorbed.

For each method the same quantities apply. The third method usually achieves the best results, and whichever method is used, the basic pilaf can be enriched with a variety of additional ingredients.

Pilafs of rice and bulgur can be prepared by any of the three methods mentioned. Pilafs made with fırık (toasted unripe wheat), döğme (pounded ripe wheat) and couscous should be cooked according to the instructions in the recipes.

POINTS TO BEAR IN MIND WHEN PREPARING A PILAF

1 For a fine pilaf you must use a high grade rice (long-grain rice or Basmati).

2 The rice should not be younger than six months. Older rice can absorb a lot of water, so it is easier to cook older rice.

3 The rice must be soaked first in salted warm water and left until the water is cool to remove excess starch. If you are in a hurry it can be washed well in hot water and left to soak for 5 minutes.

4 Stock added to a pilaf should always be boiling.

5 While cooking, pilaf must never be stirred unless it is stated explicitly in the recipe.

6 For bulgur pilaf use the bulgur straight from the packet.

7 For döğme pilaf soak the döğme first for 8 hours.

8 Precook any other ingredients to be added to a pilaf.

◊ KAŞGAR PILAVI ◊
KASHGAR PILAF

Kashgar pilaf is named after the Central Asian town where it originated.

TO SERVE 4–6
250g/8oz rice
500g/1lb shoulder of lamb, cubed
25g/1oz currants
100g/3½oz butter
50g/2oz pine nuts
200g/7oz onions, sliced
200g/7oz carrots, cut into matchsticks
½tsp ground cinnamon
¼tsp ground cloves
¼tsp ground cardamom
salt to taste
600ml/1 pint boiling stock

Soak the rice in warm water and allow to cool. Soak the currants in warm water for 30 minutes and drain. Dry-cook the meat in a covered pan for about 10 minutes until it absorbs its juices.

Melt the butter, fry the pine nuts for 2–3 minutes until golden brown, add the onions and fry for 4 minutes, then add the carrots and stir for 2 minutes. Add the currants, spices and salt and mix.

Wash the rice until the water runs clear, strain. Mix some into the pan with the meat, then add a layer of vegetables, spread on some more rice, and so on, until the rice and vegetables are used up. End with the rice. Put a plate on top to ensure the layers stay in place. Pour the stock slowly down the side of the pan. Cover and cook on medium heat until it starts to boil, then turn the heat very low and continue cooking for 20–25 minutes until the liquid is absorbed. Remove the plate, cover with absorbent paper or a cloth and replace the lid. Leave for a further 15 minutes on very low heat, then invert the pilaf on to a serving dish.

NOTE: You can also prepare this pilaf by cooking the meat and the pilaf separately then putting them in layers in a mould and cooking in a preheated oven at 250°C/500°F/gas mark 10 for 5–10 minutes. If you follow this method, cook the carrot mixture in 50ml/2fl oz of water until the liquid is absorbed, then mix with the rice.

◊ TAVUKLU PILAV ◊
RICE PILAF WITH CHICKEN

This is a favourite dish throughout Turkey.

In the Aegean region, and in Izmir in particular it has an important place in the local marriage folklore. On the day of the wedding the bride's mother prepares a tray of rice pilaf with a whole boiled chicken on top, a tray of böreks (p.129), a tray of baklava (p.136), and two simits (p.162), all covered with satin cloth, and sends them to her prospective son-in-law's home for the newly-weds to eat on their nuptial night.

Every dish in this meal has a particular significance. The chicken is meant to convey the thought that "our daughter has ceased to be ours; she now begins her new life in your home and she is henceforth yours". The rice pilaf expresses the hope that she will bear many children. The simits and böreks, made of flour, signify a life blessed with plenty. And baklava conveys the wish that their new life together may continue in an atmosphere of sweetness.

TO SERVE 6–8
1 chicken (1kg/2lb)
rice pilaf, salma fashion (p.119)
200ml/7fl oz chicken stock (p.37)
¼tsp ground cardamom
½ quantity sauce for çebiç (p.60) prepared without onion and garlic

25g/1oz butter

Boil the chicken as for arabacı soup (p.37) and remove it from the liquid.

Cook the pilaf in the chicken stock with the cardamom.

While the pilaf is resting in its steam, brush the chicken inside and out with the çebiç sauce, place it in a greased baking dish in a preheated oven at 200°C/400°F/gas mark 6, and roast for about 10 minutes, until the surface is golden brown.

Pile the pilaf in a serving dish, put the chicken on top and serve hot.

NOTE: Instead of roasting the chicken at the end, the meat may be boned and cut into small pieces and placed on the pilaf.

◊ BULGUR PILAVI ◊ KAVURMA YÖNTEMI

BULGUR PILAF KAVURMA FASHION

The discovery of bulgur grains at the 7–8,000-year-old Çatalhöyük archaeological site raises the question as to whether they used to make bulgur pilaf during that far distant period. Since the other basic ingredients are fat and water, we can presume they did. I like to think of sharing a taste for bulgur with fellow humans who lived long ago.

TO SERVE 4
250g/8oz bulgur
75g/3oz butter or cooking fat
100g/3½oz onions, finely chopped
50g/2oz thin green peppers, chopped
200g/7oz tomatoes, peeled, deseeded and chopped
½tsp salt or to taste
500ml/17fl oz stock

FOR THE GARNISH
a few sprigs of mint, chopped

Heat the butter in a two-handled pan, add the onions and fry for 5 minutes. Add the peppers and fry for 3 minutes. Add the bulgur and fry for 4–5 minutes, stirring. Add the tomatoes and fry for another 4–5 minutes. Sprinkle with salt, pour on the boiling stock and cover the pan. Cook for 3 minutes on medium heat, then 10–15 minutes on low heat, until the bulgur absorbs the liquid and holes appear on the surface. Then reduce to very low heat. Place a cloth between the pan and the lid and leave for 20 minutes. Stir with a perforated ladle, by lifting gently from the bottom of the pan and turning over. Cover the pan and leave for 10 minutes more. Serve sprinkled with chopped mint.

◊ ETLI DÖĞME PILAVI ◊

DÖĞME PILAF WITH LAMB

TO SERVE 4
150g/5oz döğme (p.119)
50g/2oz chickpeas
250g/8oz medium fat shoulder of lamb, cut into 2.5cm/1 inch cubes
1 onion, quartered
salt
50g/2oz butter
½tsp ground black pepper

Pick over the döğme and chickpeas, wash and soak in separate bowls of water for 8 hours.

Put the meat in a pan with 1L/1¾ pints water and the onion. Wash the chickpeas, add and bring slowly to the boil, then simmer for 1–1½ hours until the meat and chickpeas are tender. Add salt and cook for another 5 minutes. (If the liquid has reduced too much, top up to 500ml/17fl oz.)

Wash the döğme, drain, add to the meat and chickpeas in the pan. Cook for 5 minutes on medium heat, then 25–30 minutes on low heat. When the döğme has absorbed the liquid and forms holes on the surface, heat the butter and pour gently over it. Cover with absorbent paper or a cloth and the lid. Leave on very low heat for 20 minutes, then remove from the heat. Gently stir with a perforated ladle, and leave for another 10 minutes.

Arrange the pilaf on a heated serving dish, sprinkle with black pepper and serve hot.

◊ FIRIK PILAVI ◊

PILAF OF FIRIK

Pilaf made with firik is a speciality of Gaziantep. Firik is obtained by setting fire to fields of unripe wheat and collecting the roasted grain. This pilaf is prepared with a mixture of two-thirds firik and one third bulgur so it is not hard. Diced or minced meat may be added.

TO SERVE 4–6
100g/3½oz firik
50g/2oz bulgur
50g/2oz butter
100g/3½oz onions, finely chopped
600ml/1 pint stock
½tsp ground black pepper
¼tsp salt or to taste

Heat half the butter in a pan, add the onions and fry gently until golden. Add the stock.

Pick over the firik and bulgur. When the stock begins to boil, add the grains, cover the pan and cook for 5 minutes on high heat, 15–20 minutes on medium heat, thereafter on low heat until the firik and bulgur absorb all the liquid and holes form on the surface.

Heat the remaining butter in a small pan, add the black pepper and immediately pour over the pilaf. Taste and add salt if necessary. Cover with absorbent paper or a cloth, replace the lid, and leave on very low heat (use a heat diffuser if necessary) for 20 minutes. Stir gently with a perforated ladle. Cover again and leave for another 5 minutes. Serve hot.

◊ PERDELI PILAV ◊

"VEILED" PILAF

Perdeli pilaf is a special pilaf prepared in Siirt. With its decorative "veiled" appearance it is the *pièce de résistance* on all wedding menus. It is brought to the table in its mould and then turned out on to the serving dish.

TO SERVE 8–10
1kg/2lb cooked chicken, cut into largish pieces
rice pilaf (p.119)
25g/1oz butter
25g/1oz shelled almonds
100g/3½oz chicken liver
1tsp ground allspice
½tsp ground black pepper
½tsp ground cinnamon
¼tsp ground cardamom
FOR THE "VEIL"
1 egg, beaten
25ml/1fl oz yoghurt
½tsp salt
150g/5oz flour
olive oil
TO GREASE THE MOULD
25g/1oz butter
100g/3½oz split almonds
ovenproof mould with a lid, approx 18cm/7in deep and 25cm/10in in diameter

Cook the rice pilaf in chicken stock.

Melt the butter in a pan, and fry the almonds for 3–4 minutes until golden. Chop the liver into pieces smaller than the almonds, add and fry for 4–5 minutes, until the liver is cooked. Stir in the spices and remove from the heat. Slowly mix into the hot pilaf. Leave to rest for 10 minutes in a covered pan, then stir and put to one side.

Mix together the egg, yoghurt and salt. Add the flour and enough olive oil to make a smooth dough. Knead briefly, then cover and allow to rest for 20 minutes.

Grease the mould and its lid with the butter. Stick the almonds in a decorative pattern on the buttered inner surface, and on the lid. Leave to set in the refrigerator.

Set aside a quarter of the dough. Roll out the remainder thinly and line the mould with it. Fill the mould with alternate layers of chicken and rice, pressing down lightly with the back of a spoon. Roll out half the unused dough and cover the pilaf. Put on the lid. With the remaining piece of dough seal the mould all round the edge of the lid to ensure it is airtight. Cook in the oven at 200°C/400°F/gas mark 6 for 40–45 minutes until the dough turns golden.

Remove the lid, turn out on to a serving dish and serve. (If the food sticks to the mould, it means it has not cooked enough, so return to the oven for a little longer.)

◊ ÜZLEMELI PILAV ◊

PILAF WITH CHICKPEAS, LAMB AND SULTANAS

Üzlemeli pilaf is served at wedding receptions in Şanlı Urfa in southeastern Anatolia. In the rest of Turkey, wedding pilafs are usually garnished with sweet-meats or zerde (p.149), but the people of Şanlı Urfa prefer this recipe.

TO SERVE 4
rice pilaf (p.119)
FOR THE ÜZLEME
50g/2oz chickpeas
50g/2oz sultanas
125g/4oz lean shoulder of lamb
50g/2oz pekmez (grape syrup p.173)
¼tsp ground cinnamon
¼tsp ground black pepper
¼tsp salt

Pick over and wash the chickpeas, soak for 8 hours, then wash again and add to 500ml/ 17fl oz cold water. Boil for approximately 50 minutes until tender, then strain.

Pick over and wash the sultanas, soak in warm water for 30 minutes.

Dice the meat the same size as the chickpeas, and dry-cook gently in a covered pan for about 10 minutes until it absorbs its juices. When it begins to sizzle, add 400ml/ 14fl oz boiling water and cover. Bring to the boil, reduce to low heat and cook for nearly 1 hour, until the meat is tender. Then add the chickpeas and sultanas, return to the boil and add the grape syrup. Cook for another 15 minutes until the chickpeas and meat soak up the syrup. Sprinkle with cinnamon, black pepper and salt, cook for a further 5 minutes, then remove from the heat.

While the meat is cooking, prepare the pilaf. Put it on a heated serving dish, pour over the hot üzleme and serve at once.

◊ DOMATESLI KUSKUS ◊

COUSCOUS WITH TOMATO SAUCE

TO SERVE 10–12
FOR THE PILAF
1L/1¾ pints water
1tbsp salt
½tsp olive oil
250g/8oz couscous
FOR THE SAUCE
25g/1oz butter
150g/5oz onions, finely sliced
200g/7oz tomatoes, peeled, deseeded and chopped

½tsp ground black pepper
½tsp salt
200ml/7fl oz hot water
FOR THE GARNISH
25g/1oz butter
1 sage leaf

Bring the water to the boil with the salt and olive oil, add the couscous, and cover the pan. Bring to the boil again, then simmer for 10 minutes. Drain.

While cooking the couscous, melt the

butter in another pan. Add the onions and fry for 6–7 minutes until soft. Add the tomatoes and fry for 8–10 minutes until they absorb their juices. Sprinkle with the black pepper and salt, add the water and cover the pan. Bring to the boil, turn the heat very low and cook for 5 minutes.

Add the couscous to the sauce, mix well,

cover and cook for 3 minutes on medium heat and a further 15 minutes on low heat.

In a frying pan heat the butter with the sage leaf. Pour gently over the couscous and leave, covered, for another 15 minutes, over a heat diffuser.

Turn the couscous out on to a heated dish and serve.

◊ YUFKALI IÇ PILAVI ◊
SPICED PILAF WRAPPED IN YUFKA

Iç pilavı is one of the finest and tastiest of all pilafs. It may be served on its own or wrapped in yufka (thin sheets of dough like filo), as below.

TO SERVE 4–6
300g/10oz rice
25g/1oz currants
150g/5oz butter
25g/1oz pine nuts
100g/3½oz onions, finely chopped
200g/7oz lamb's liver, finely chopped
100g/3½oz tomatoes, peeled, sliced and deseeded or 25g/1oz tomato purée
¼tsp ground black pepper
¼tsp red pepper
¼tsp ground cinnamon
¼tsp ground allspice
⅛tsp ground cardamom
1tsp salt
1 tsp caster sugar
TO WRAP THE PILAF
1 quantity of yufka (p.127)

Grease a shallow pan or mould measuring about 20 × 8 × 6cm/8 × 3 × 2 inches and set aside.

Soak the rice in warm salted water and allow to cool. Soak the currants for 30 minutes in warm water.

Melt 25g/1oz butter and fry the pine nuts for 1–2 minutes, stirring, until they darken. Add the onions and fry for 3 minutes until golden. Add the liver and fry for 4 minutes, then add the tomatoes and fry for another 4 minutes or add the tomato purée. Add the drained currants, spices, salt, sugar and 600ml/1 pint water and bring slowly to the boil.

Meanwhile, heat the remaining butter, add the thoroughly washed and drained rice, and fry for 4–5 minutes, stirring. When the rice begins to stick to the bottom of the pan, add the boiling mixture from the other pan. Cover and cook for 5 minutes on medium heat and 15–20 minutes on low heat until the rice absorbs the liquid and holes appear on the surface. Place a sheet of absorbent paper or a cloth over the pan. Replace the lid and leave for 20 minutes on very low heat. Stir gently, then leave to cool, uncovered.

Carefully spread the yufka in the prepared pan or mould, letting it hang over the edges. Fill with the pilaf. Fold over the edges of the yufka, making sure the rice is completely enclosed. Brush with butter and bake in a preheated oven at 250°C/500°F/gas mark 10 for 5–10 minutes, until the yufka turns golden.

Invert carefully on to a serving dish and serve hot.

◊

BREAD, BOREKS AND NOODLES

◊

◊ EKMEKLER ◊
BREAD

Bread is a staple food in Turkey; a Turk will eat as much bread in a day as an English or American person would eat in a week. Bread is also revered as one of the foods sent down to earth by God's command, according to the Koran. Because bread is valued so highly not a crumb is allowed to go to waste, and a number of dishes have been devised to use up bread.

At the imperial palace in Istanbul, three types of bread used to be baked — fodla – slightly leavened flat bread, has ekmek – fine white bread, and somun ekmek – ordinary bread. Fodla was served at the sultan's table, has ekmek to the ladies of the harem and the palace dignitaries, and somun ekmek to the lower-ranking members of the household. They also had simit – ring-shaped rolls with sesame seeds; gevrek – ring-shaped crisp bread; çörek – savoury round buns; and many types of börek – savoury or sweet pies. All of these are still to be had today; in addition, pitta especially is baked in great quantities during the month of Ramadan, because everyone likes to break the daily fast with the best kind of bread. Simits are made with bread dough, shaped in a ring, dipped in sesame seeds and baked. You will find them for sale on every city street. Yufka (below) and other breads are still made at home in Anatolia.

◊ YUFKA EKMEĞI ◊
UNLEAVENED FLATBREAD

TO MAKE 12 YUFKA
50g/2oz strong plain flour
50g/2oz plain flour
25g/1oz wholemeal flour
½tsp salt
100ml/3½fl oz warm water

Mix all the flours and salt in a bowl, gradually add the water and knead to a firm dough. Divide into 12 pieces and leave to rest for 30 minutes covered with a damp cloth on a tray sprinkled with flour. The longer you leave the dough the better it is. Roll out each piece on a floured board with a long, thin rolling pin. The circles of dough should be no thicker than 3mm/⅛ inch.

Heat a griddle or a non-stick frying pan until very hot and cook the yufka briefly on both sides. Once cooked, the yufka can be stacked and kept for several weeks in a dry place.

When a yufka is to be eaten, sprinkle warm water over it, fold it in half, wrap in a cloth and leave for 30 minutes so that it becomes soft and pliable.

When yufka bread is rolled up and stuffed with a filling, it is called a dürüm (the word means roll). Cold vegetables or herbs make popular fillings; you could use all the salads in this book with a small amount of dressing; or try mirtoğa with honey (p.43), or various kinds of helvas. Still simpler is to spread a little butter on the yufka, put honey or cheese on it and then roll it up – an instant snack.

◊ ET TIRIDI ◊

LAMB ON CROÛTONS

A snack served on toast or croûtons is called a tırıt.

TO SERVE 4–6
600g/1¼lb medium fat shoulder of lamb on the bone
1L/1¾ pints meat stock (p.33)
150g/5oz onions, sliced
1tsp salt
125g/4oz wholemeal bread or old white bread, cubed
1tsp sumac (p.173)
a few sprigs of parsley, chopped

Cook the meat in the stock for approximately 2 hours on low heat until tender, strain. If the liquid has reduced, top up to 500ml/17fl oz with hot water. Remove the meat from the bone and return to the stock.

Sprinkle the onions with salt, leave for 4 minutes, then rub with your fingers, wash and squeeze out any juice. Toast white bread briefly in the oven – wholemeal bread should not be toasted.

Put the bread in a serving dish, cover with the onions and sprinkle with sumac. Test the temperature of the meat with your finger. If it is slightly too hot to bear, pour the contents of the pan over the bread. (If it is *too* hot the bread becomes doughy, if too cool it becomes tasteless). Sprinkle with parsley and serve immediately.

◊ KELEDOS ◊

LAMB AND VEGETABLES ON CROÛTONS

T his dish comes from Van in eastern Turkey. It can also be served as a soup without the bread.

TO SERVE 4–6
50g/2oz chickpeas
125g/4oz green lentils
125g/4oz lamb on the bone
50g/2oz bulgur
250g/8oz leeks, thinly sliced
250g/8oz potatoes, peeled and cubed
salt to taste
1½ quantities yoghurt and garlic sauce (p.172)
125g/4oz day-old bread, cubed and toasted in the oven
100g/3½oz melted butter

Soak the chickpeas and lentils for 7–8 hours. Drain and boil in fresh water for 30 minutes. Strain.

Put the meat, parboiled chickpeas and lentils and the bulgur in 1L/1¾ pints water, bring to the boil and simmer for about 1 hour, until the meat and chickpeas are tender. If necessary add more hot water.

Add the leeks, cook for 10 minutes, then add the potatoes and cook for about 15 minutes, until done. Add salt and cook for 5 minutes, then remove from the heat.

Prepare the yoghurt and garlic sauce and add to the pan, stirring very slowly.

Put the toasted bread cubes in a serving dish. Pour over the hot meat and vegetables and drizzle over the melted butter. Serve hot.

◊ BÖREKLER ◊
S A V O U R Y   P A S T I E S

Böreks are one of the greatest achievements of Turkish cuisine and one of the oldest, having come from Central Asia when the Turks migrated westwards. There is an endless variety of böreks bearing different names, according to the way they are prepared. They are all made with layers of flaky or filo pastry and butter and have fillings based on meat or cheese. Böreks may be served as a course in a main meal, as a snack during the day, and especially at teatime. If you haven't the time to make the dough, bought filo pastry can be used instead.

◊ SIGARA BÖREĞİ ◊
C I G A R E T T E   B Ö R E K

TO SERVE 6
½ quantity börek filling of your choice (p.130)
3 yufka (p.127) or 2 sheets of filo pastry
olive or sunflower oil for deep frying

Prepare the filling.

Cut each yufka into 4. Place some filling along the long side of each piece of yufka. Fold the edge over the filling, tuck in the ends and roll like a cigarette. Brush some water on the join to ensure it sticks and fry in very hot oil for 5 minutes. Drain on absorbent paper, then serve hot.

◊ SU BÖREĞİ ◊
B Ö R E K S   S T U F F E D   W I T H   M E A T   O R   C H E E S E

Layers of wafer-thin dough spread with butter form a sandwich around a meat or cheese filling. Like baklava, börck is baked in a large flat tin and divided into portions.

Su böreği is the most famous and one of the best böreks. The kind available from a market stall is often rather stodgy, whereas the homemade version is deliciously light, prepared the way described below. Su böreği cooked on a blackened brazier, using oak wood charcoal as in Konya homes, has a unique taste not to be found in any other kind of börek.

TO SERVE 20
250g/8oz strong plain flour
250g/8oz self-raising flour
5 eggs
salt
100g/3½oz strong plain flour
100g/3½oz wheat starch (p.173)
250g/8oz butter
1tbsp olive oil or sunflower oil

FOR THE MEAT FILLING
25g/1oz currants
25g/1oz pine nuts
25g/1oz butter
200g/7oz onions
250g/8oz shoulder of lamb, minced
a few sprigs of parsley, chopped
½tsp salt
½tsp ground black pepper
½tsp ground cinnamon
FOR THE CHEESE FILLING
250g/8oz white cheese, grated or crumbled
25g/1oz parsley
1 egg (optional)

To prepare the meat filling, soak the currants in warm water for 30 minutes and drain. Fry the pine nuts in the butter for 3–4 minutes until golden. Parboil the onions, drain, chop finely, add to the nuts and fry for 2 minutes. Add the lamb and fry until the meat absorbs its juices, then add the parsley, salt, black pepper and cinnamon. Mix in the currants and remove from the heat.

To prepare the cheese filling, mix the cheese with the parsley. Mix in the egg if you are using one. If the cheese is not salted, add a little salt.

To prepare the börek, grease a 35–40cm/ 15–16 inch baking tin.

Sift the first two quantities of flour on to a pastry board. Make a hollow in the middle, and add the eggs, 75ml/3fl oz water and 1tbsp salt. Draw the flour in from the edges. Knead for 15 minutes to make a firm dough. Divide the dough into 12 pieces and place on a flour-sprinkled tray. Cover with a damp cloth and leave to rest for at least 30 minutes – the longer the better.

Mix together the equal quantities of flour and wheat starch. Roll out the pieces of dough as thinly as possible with a long,

thin rolling pin (called an oklava), sprinkling each side in turn with the flour and starch mixture; set aside two of the best sheets of dough for the underside and the top of the börek. Line the tin with one. Place the remainder, sprinkled with a very little flour, on top of each other and cut them into quarters.

Melt the butter in a pan and pour off the clear fat, leaving the sediment at the bottom.

Put 3L/4¼ pints water, 2tbsp salt and the oil in a large pan and bring to the boil. Drop the dough quarters into the water in batches, and boil for 1–2 minutes. When they float up to the surface, remove with a skimmer and drop into cold water. Drain thoroughly on a cloth, then layer in the baking tin, pouring 1tbsp of clarified butter over every two or three layers. When you have used up half the dough, spread with the cheese or meat filling. Continue boiling the remaining sheets of dough and adding more layers as before. Then cover with the remaining one large sheet set aside for the purpose. Trim the edges, brush with the remaining clarified butter and cut into squares with a sharp knife. Bake in a preheated oven, 260°C/500°F/gas mark 10 for 25–30 minutes.

Serve the böreks straight from the tin.

◊ ÇİĞ BÖREK ◊

BÖREK WITH RAW MEAT STUFFING

Çiğ börek is certainly of ancient Asian origin. The Tatar Turks still make it to this day and theirs is the best way. It is easy to make and tasty.

The classic way is to stuff the börek with raw meat (some people call them "raw böreks"), but I prefer to cook it a little, as in this recipe, because the filling does not then make the dough soggy.

It can be served cold for picnics.

TO SERVE 10
1 egg
150ml/¼ pint water
1tsp salt
250g/8oz strong plain flour
olive oil or sunflower oil for deep frying
FOR THE FILLING
150g/5oz shoulder of lamb, minced
50g/2oz onions, chopped
150g/5oz tomatoes, peeled, deseeded and chopped
½tsp ground black pepper
½tsp salt
a few sprigs of parsley, chopped

Prepare the filling first. Put all the ingredients except the parsley in a pan, dry-fry for 2–3 minutes, stirring, and remove from the heat. The mixture will be partly cooked. Add the parsley, mix, and leave to cool.

For the börek, beat the egg, water and salt with a whisk, then add the flour and blend to a soft dough. Knead on a floured board for 5 minutes. Divide into 20 pieces, and leave to rest for 20 minutes on a floured tray covered with a damp cloth.

Roll out each piece on a well floured board with a short thick rolling pin into 5mm/¼ inch yufka. Divide the filling between them, fold over, and seal the edge by pressing firmly with the fingers.

Heat the oil and deep-fry the böreks for 3 minutes each. Drain on absorbent paper, and serve hot or cold.

◊ SAÇ BÖREĞİ ◊

GRIDDLE-COOKED CHEESE BÖREK

Saç böreği is a speciality of Konya. It is cooked on a flat iron pan or griddle over a very low fire. The cheese used for this kind of börek must be very dry; a "wet" cheese would make the wafer-thin yufka dough disintegrate.

If you wish, you can cut this börek in half after filling and cook it in a nonstick frying pan, but take care not to overcook it or it will be dry.

TO SERVE 12
1 quantity cheese filling (p.130)
1 quantity dough for yufka bread (p.127)
ACCOMPANIMENTS
25g/1oz butter
ayran (p.168)

Prepare the cheese filling, then prepare the dough and divide into 12 pieces. Place them on a floured tray, cover with a damp cloth and allow to rest for 30 minutes.

Roll out each piece of dough with a long thin rolling pin on a floured pastry board or marble slab. Place some of the filling in the middle of one half of each dough circle and fold over the other half. Press the edges firmly with your fingers to close the börek. Cook at once on a griddle or in a nonstick frying pan for 2-3 minutes on each side.

Butter the cooked böreks as they become ready, and stack them up in a covered pan. When all are cooked, close the pan, put a heavy cloth (in Turkey we would use a small rug) over it and leave for 5 minutes before serving with ayran.

◊ PUF BÖREĞİ ◊

PUFFED BÖREK

This börek is easy to make and can be prepared with a variety of different fillings. Puffed börek is always taken on picnics in Anatolia.

TO MAKE 20
½tsp butter
1 egg
100ml/3½fl oz water
a few drops vinegar
1tsp salt
100g/3½oz strong plain flour
100g/3½oz self-raising flour
50g/2oz butter, melted and cooled

250g/8oz cooking fat or butter or olive oil or sunflower oil for deep-frying
FOR THE FILLING
1 quantity meat or cheese filling (p.130)

Prepare the börek filling.

To make the dough, melt the butter and pour into a bowl with the egg, water, vinegar and salt. Mix well, add both flours and knead to a smooth dough. Divide into two lumps, place them on a floured tray and allow to rest for 20 minutes under a damp cloth. On a floured pastry board roll out one of the lumps of dough to a thick strip with a long, thin rolling pin. Brush half the melted butter along the middle. Roll up into a cylinder, then cut it into 10 pieces. Take each piece with both hands and press inwards. Prepare the second lump of dough in the same way. Allow to rest for 30 minutes on a floured surface under a damp cloth.

Roll out each small piece of dough with a short thick rolling pin to a 5mm/¼ inch strip. Divide the filling between the strips, fold the dough over, press the edges to seal and trim with a pastry cutter to make a decorative edge.

Deep-fry the böreks for 3 minutes in hot fat or oil, and transfer to absorbent paper. Place the böreks on a serving dish and serve hot. They can be eaten cold as well but are tastier when hot.

◊ HAŞHAŞLI KATMER ◊
POPPY-SEED PASTRIES

Plain katmer – brushed with oil but without the sprinkling of poppy seeds – is traditionally a sacred food that can be distributed instead of pişi on Kandil feast days. After the oil is brushed on, the katmer is folded into a cylindrical shape, then flattened with a rolling pin and fried in oil.

Of the many kinds of katmer popular in Turkey, the haşhaşli katmer is the best loved in the hinterland of the Aegean region where poppies generally grow in large quantities. It has a delicious flavour.

FOR 2 KATMERS
50g/2oz strong plain flour
50g/2oz self-raising flour
¼tsp salt
1 egg
25ml/1fl oz water
poppy seed or sunflower oil for frying
FOR THE FILLING
100g/3½oz poppy seeds
100ml/3½fl oz poppy seed or sunflower oil
ACCOMPANIMENT
pekmez (grape syrup – p.173) or honey

To make the filling, roast the poppy seeds in a dry frying pan until they darken. Crush to a thick paste in a mortar. Mix in the oil.

Sift both flours into a bowl, sprinkle on the salt, make a well in the centre and add the egg and water. Starting from the middle, knead the dough until silky and soft. Divide in two and leave to rest on a floured board for 20 minutes.

Roll each piece out as thinly as possible on a well floured surface. Brush half of the poppy seed mixture on each katmer leaving 1.25cm/½ inch border clear. Fold both sides of the katmer into the middle. Repeat to make a parcel. Seal the edges by pressing firmly.

Fry the katmer in poppy seed or sunflower oil on medium heat for 1 minute each side, then turn again and fry the first side for another minute. They should be gold rather than brown. Lay on absorbent paper to drain, then transfer to a pan with a lid, cover and leave for 5 minutes.

Place the katmer on a serving dish and serve with pekmez or honey.

NOTE: Tahinli katmer – tahina pastries – can be prepared in the same way.

◊ MANTI ◊

TURKISH RAVIOLI IN YOGHURT SAUCE

Mantı are prepared throughout Anatolia, and the city of Kayseri (the ancient Caesarea) is especially famous for them. To the people of Kayseri pastırma – spiced, cured meat – and mantı are as popular a feature of their diet as anchovies among the natives of the Black Sea region.

TO SERVE 4–6
25g/1oz butter
500ml/17fl oz stock (p.33)
1½ measures yoghurt and garlic sauce (p.172)
FOR THE FILLING
100g/3½oz lean lamb, minced
25g/1oz onion, finely chopped
1tbsp chopped parsley
¼tsp salt
¼tsp ground black pepper
FOR THE PASTA
1 egg
125g/4oz strong plain flour
½tsp salt
25–50ml/1–2fl oz water
FOR THE GARNISH
50g/2oz butter
2 sage leaves
¼tsp mint or red pepper

Grease a shallow round oven dish with 25g/1oz butter and set aside.

To make the filling, put the ingredients in a bowl and mix well.

To make the pasta, break the egg into another bowl, stir in the flour and salt, then gradually add the water to make a dough. Knead for 10 minutes. Divide the dough into two, cover with a damp cloth and allow to rest for 30 minutes. Roll out with a long thin rolling pin to 3mm/⅛ inch thickness. Cut into 2.5cm/1 inch squares. Place a little filling in the middle of each, fold over all four corners loosely so that the filling is still visible and pinch the tips together to make mantıs.

Place the mantıs in the oven dish. Bake, uncovered, in a preheated oven at 200°C/400°F/gas mark 6 for about 25 minutes, until the pasta becomes golden. Remove from the oven.

Bring the stock to the boil and ladle over the mantıs. Cover the dish, return to the oven and cook for a further 15 minutes or until the mantıs absorb the liquid and are tender.

Prepare the yoghurt and garlic sauce and the pasta. Pour the sauce over the mantıs. Melt the butter with the sage leaves, then add the mint or red pepper and remove from the heat in under 1 minute. Take out the sage and pour gently over the yoghurt and serve hot.

NOTE: Alternatively, boil the mantıs in stock, toss them in the yoghurt sauce and drizzle with melted butter.

◊

DESSERTS

◊

◊ TATLILAR ◊
DESSERTS

"Let us have a sweet dish, let us indulge in sweet talk."

TURKISH PROVERB

Turkish cuisine is rich in desserts and sweets. From the cradle to the grave, Turks insist on a sweet to mark any occasion. This custom is carried so far that, traditional anniversaries apart, someone starting a new job would mark the occasion by presenting sweets to relatives, friends and colleagues; the arrival of a friend from distant parts would be celebrated by exchanging gifts of sweets; someone moving into a new house would entertain neighbours with a sweet dish; and a gift for a friend would always include a box of sweets. So it goes on, and in Turkey there is always an excuse to have something sweet.

Many desserts and sweets have an interesting historical background. Some are described in detail in the Classical Turkish Dictionary. During the Ottoman period the makers of sweet dishes and pastry cooks organized themselves into a number of associations too numerous to list here, each one specializing in a particular expertise, such as making sherbets, or fritters, or milk puddings, or helvas, or confectionery. In those days the Turks were far ahead of their neighbours in this respect. Today confectioners, pastry cooks, makers of milk desserts and all the others continue to ply their trade and sell their wares from specialist shops and on street corners. The quality of their goods is usually very high, but of course nothing quite competes with homemade desserts.

◊ BAKLAVA ◊
BAKLAVA

Baklava is perhaps *the* national dessert, and it is served at official functions and at all kinds of banquets and parties. Although excellent baklava is made in private houses, the special baklava shops of Gaziantep in southeastern Turkey achieve such high standards that even homemade baklava seldom surpasses them. Gaziantep is the very mecca of baklava making, as it is of kebab making.

Several other desserts with descriptive names are made with baklava pastry: Bülbül Yuvası – Nightingale's Nest; Kocakarı Gerdanı – Old Woman's Neck; and Dilber Dudağı – Beautiful Woman's Lips.

You can substitute 250g/8oz bought filo pastry if you like.

TO SERVE 16
FOR THE FILLING
75g/3oz shelled walnuts, pistachio nuts or almonds
1tbsp caster sugar
FOR THE PASTRY
125g/4oz strong plain white flour
125g/4oz self-raising flour
1 egg
150ml/¼ pint warm water
1tsp salt
100g/3½oz wheat starch (p.173)
250g/8oz butter, melted
a small cube of bread

FOR THE SYRUP
375g/12oz caster sugar
250ml/8fl oz water
1tbsp lemon juice

Grease a 25cm/10 inch baking dish with a little melted butter. To prepare the filling, crush the walnuts and mix with the sugar. If you are using pistachios or almonds, blanch for 1 minute, remove the skins and when thoroughly dry crush and mix with the sugar.

To make the pastry, sieve the flours into a bowl, make a hollow in the middle, and add the egg, water and salt. Prepare a soft dough by drawing the flour into the middle and mixing well. Knead on a pastry board or marble slab for 15–20 minutes, repeatedly pressing outwards with the heel of your hand to stretch the dough, and then folding it over. If it sticks to your hand, dredge with a very little flour, but it's better if you can avoid it. The dough is ready when, holding it at one end, you can lift it and it stretches without breaking. Divide into 20 pieces, and allow to rest for at least 1 hour, and preferably 2–3 hours, on a floured board under two layers of damp cloth.

Roll out each piece of dough into a very thin yufka, sprinkling wheat starch on both sides. Remove excess with a pastry brush. Layer half the yufka or sheets of filo in the baking dish, brushing each layer with a very little melted butter. Spread the filling on the pastry, then cover with the remainder of the yufka, buttering each layer lightly as before. Cut the baklava into small squares or diamonds with a sharp knife, wiping the blade after each cut so that it doesn't stick.

Put the remaining butter and the bread in a pan and heat gently. When the bread becomes pale yellow and hardens (it must not become golden), remove from the heat. Skim off any scum, and leave until the sediment settles. Pour the clear butter into another pan and wait until it cools sufficiently to be bearable to the fingertip.

Now gently pour the butter over the baklava, leaving no parts dry. To allow the layers to absorb it, leave to stand for 30 minutes at room temperature. Then bake for 35 minutes in a preheated oven at 200°C/400°F/gas mark 6.

Shortly before removing the baklava from the oven, prepare the syrup. Heat the sugar, water and lemon juice in a pan, stirring until the sugar melts. When the syrup begins to boil, lower the heat, cook for 2 minutes, then remove from the heat. Allow to rest for 5 minutes. Take the baklava out of the oven and allow to rest for 5 minutes, then pour the syrup over it, leaving no area uncovered. Cool and serve the baklava in the baking dish.

◊ REVANI ◊
SEMOLINA DESSERT

Revani is a delicious light dessert that is easy to prepare.

TO SERVE 8–12
FOR THE REVANI
100g/3½oz self-raising flour

100g/3½oz semolina
100g/3½oz caster sugar
6 eggs
FOR THE SYRUP
600g/1¼lb caster sugar

500ml/17fl oz water
1tbsp lemon juice
FOR THE TOPPING
250g/8oz kaymak (p.173), clotted cream or whipped double cream

Grease a pan that is 25cm/10 inches in diameter and 5–6cm/2–2½ inches deep. Sieve the flour into a bowl and mix with the semolina. Put the sugar and eggs into another bowl and whisk until smooth and thick. Add the flour and semolina mixture and mix carefully. Pour into the pan and bake in a preheated oven at 175°C/350°F/ gas mark 6 for 25–30 minutes until the top is lightly browned.

While the revani is baking, make the syrup. Put the sugar, water and lemon juice in a pan over medium heat, and stir until the sugar melts. Boil for 2 minutes and remove from the heat.

Cut the revani into squares. Pour the hot syrup over them and return to the oven for 1 minute. Leave for several hours to cool and absorb the syrup.

Top with kaymak or clotted cream just before serving.

◊ GÖZLEME TATLISI ◊

PANCAKES

Although pancakes are found in Istanbul cuisine, their origin is very much in the provinces. In places where there were no ovens in the olden days, pancakes served instead of desserts made with pastry.

TO SERVE 4
FOR THE SYRUP
100g/3½oz caster sugar
75ml/3fl oz water
¼tsp lemon juice
FOR THE PANCAKES
50g/2oz strong plain flour
50g/2oz self-raising flour
¼tsp salt
1 egg yolk
50g/2oz melted butter
50ml/2fl oz water
FOR FRYING
50g/2oz butter
FOR THE GARNISH
25g/1oz crushed walnuts

To make the syrup, put the sugar, water and lemon juice in a pan on medium heat and stir until the sugar melts. When it comes to the boil, remove it from the heat after 30 seconds. Allow to cool.

To make the pancakes, sieve both flours and the salt into a bowl, make a hollow in the middle and put in the egg yolk, 1tsp melted butter and the water. Mix to a soft dough. Divide into four and leave to rest for 20 minutes on a floured surface under a damp cloth.

Roll out the dough as thinly as possible. Brush all over with warm melted butter and roll into a cylinder. Allow to rest again under a damp cloth for 20 minutes or until the butter hardens.

Roll out again into discs of 10–15cm/5–6 inches. Heat the butter in a frying pan and fry the pancakes for 2 minutes on each side or until golden. Lay on absorbent paper. When all the pancakes are ready, pour the syrup over them, then roll up and arrange on a serving dish. Sprinkle with the crushed walnuts.

◊ LOKMA ◊

LOKMA FRITTERS

Lokma , like pişi and katmer, is asso-ciated with religious feast days. Lokma is said to signify the seal of the Prophet Mohammed.

Very small lokmas, made with just a tea-spoon of batter, are known as saray lok-ması or palace lokma, because they are made in the manner used in the imperial palace in Ottoman times. In Izmir, which has shops that specialize in lokmas, they are shaped into rings and deep-fried.

Lokmas can be eaten either hot or cold.

TO SERVE 6
150g/5oz strong plain flour
1/2 tsp dried yeast
1/4 tsp caster sugar
4 pieces mastic, optional (p.173)
1/4 tsp salt
olive or sunflower oil for deep-frying
FOR THE SYRUP
200g/7oz granulated sugar
200ml/7fl oz water
1/4 tsp lemon juice

Prepare the syrup as described on p.138.

Dissolve the yeast in 25ml/1fl oz warm water with the sugar. Sift the flour into a bowl, make a well in the middle, add the yeast mixture and stir, drawing in the flour, to a smooth batter. Cover the surface with flour, and leave to rise in a warm spot. Crush the mastic with the salt in a mortar, if using, and sprinkle over the flour.

When the yeast starts to work and cracks appear on the surface, make a well in the middle, add 150ml/6fl oz warm water and mix thoroughly by hand. Cover again and leave in a warm place for 40–50 minutes or until the dough rises, doubling or trebling in volume.

Heat the oil. Take some dough in your fist and squeeze it out through the hole formed by the thumb and index finger. Drop into the oil and fry, occasionally prodding the lokmas with the back of a ladle. Transfer briefly to absorbent paper, then drop into cold syrup for 5 minutes.

◊ TULUMBA TATLISI ◊

CRISP-FRIED PASTRIES IN SYRUP

TO SERVE 6
FOR THE SYRUP
400g/14oz granulated sugar
300ml/½ pint water
1tsp lemon juice
FOR THE DOUGH
200ml/7fl oz water
50g/2oz butter
¼tsp salt
75g/3oz plain flour
75g/3oz strong plain flour
1tbsp fine semolina
1tbsp arrowroot
3–4 eggs
olive or sunflower oil for deep-frying

Prepare the syrup. Combine the ingredients, stirring, over medium heat, until the sugar melts. When it comes to the boil reduce the heat to very low and after 2 minutes remove from the heat and cool.

To prepare the dough, put the water, butter and salt in a heavy pan. Bring to the boil, add both flours, the semolina and arrowroot, stir once, then remove from the heat and stir thoroughly. Return the pan to a very low heat and cook for 10 minutes, stirring until the mixture is smooth and comes away from the sides of the pan. Remove from the heat and cool to lukewarm. Add the eggs one at a time, beating vigorously. The dough should be slippery and stick to your hand. Stir in 1tbsp of syrup. The syrup gives it a rosy colour when fried. Fill a pastry bag with a fluted nozzle with the dough.

Pour the oil into a pan, and while still cold squeeze into it small pieces of dough, about 4cm/1½ inches long, cutting off each strip with a knife. When the pan is half full – but no more because the pastries will double in size – place on medium heat. Keep shaking the pan gently until the pieces of pastry turn golden and rise to the surface. Reduce the heat. (If the oil gets too hot the inside remains raw.) Fry for 8–10 minutes, occasionally turning the pastries with a perforated ladle.

Fry the remaining pastries in the same way. Drain quickly on absorbent paper, then drop into the cold syrup. Leave in the syrup for 5 minutes, then serve.

NOTE: The dough can be prepared without the semolina and arrowroot, by increasing the flour to 200g/7oz. Shape into balls with a hole through the middle, fry and drop into the syrup and you have a dish called Kadın Göbeği – Lady's Navel.

If the same dough is rolled in the palm of your hand, then folded in two, fried and drenched in syrup, it is called Dilber Dudağı – Beautiful Woman's Lips. Finally, when shaped like a finger, and treated in the same way, it becomes Vezir Parmağı – Vizier's Finger.

◊ KIZ MEMESI TEL KADAYIFI ◊

"GIRL'S BREASTS"

Kadayıf, shredded pastry that looks like vermicelli, is used to make a number of classic Turkish desserts. The dough, also called konafa, can be bought from Greek and Middle Eastern shops. As with baklava, there are many ways of preparing it, and many different fillings to choose from.

TO SERVE 12
300g/10oz kadayıf (shredded pastry)
100g/3½oz butter
100ml/3½fl oz warm milk
12 walnut halves
FOR THE SYRUP
500g/1lb caster sugar
300ml/10fl oz water
1 tsp lemon juice
FOR THE FILLING
100g/3½oz shelled walnuts
1 tbsp caster sugar

To make the filling, grind or mince the nuts and mix with the sugar.

Grease a 30cm/12 inch baking pan with half the butter.

Melt the remaining butter, allow to cool and when the sediment has settled, carefully pour off the clear butter into a bowl with 1 tbsp of warm milk. Put the kadayıf on a pastry board or marble slab, and dipping your hands repeatedly in the buttery milk, rub the kadayıf with your fingers, separating the strands. Work in all of the oily milk and divide into 12 portions.

At the bottom of a teacup put half a walnut, and press on to it half a portion of kadayıf. Put 1 tbsp of filling on top and press on to it the remaining half portion of kadayıf. Turn out into the baking pan. Prepare the remaining kadayıf in the same way. Bake for 25 minutes in a preheated oven at 225°C/450°F/gas mark 8. Remove from the oven and brush the kadayıf well with the remaining milk. Cover and allow to rest for 5 minutes.

Prepare the syrup as for baklava (p.136). Gently pour the hot syrup over the kadayıf and leave for several hours. Serve cold.

◊ HOŞMERIM ◊

CREAMY WHOLEMEAL PANCAKE

Hoşmerim is of Anatolian origin. The story goes that a lady devised this dish and served it to her husband. He commended her by remarking: "This is a very nice dish," and she responded: "Hoş (nice) mu (is it) erim (husband)?" Thus the dish came to be known as "hoş-m'erim"!

You can also serve hoşmerim plain, sprinkled with icing sugar.

TO SERVE 6
150g/5oz butter
100g/4oz wholemeal flour
150g/5oz double cream or milk
2 eggs
100g/3½oz clear honey
200g/7oz kaymak (p.173) or clotted cream

Melt 75g/3oz of the butter in a nonstick frying pan and remove from the heat. Add half the flour and mix well, then return to low heat and cook for 10–15 minutes until golden.

Put the rest of the flour in a bowl, whisk in the cream or milk, then the eggs. Pour this mixture into the butter and flour, and stir with a wooden spoon for 5 minutes over low heat until it becomes grainy instead of sticking to the frying pan. Remove from the heat and turn the mixture into a smaller frying pan. Compress the hoşmerim firmly with the back of a spoon to fit the pan. Return to very low heat and fry the underside for 4–5 minutes (the top must not be fried) slipping in more butter as required down the sides of the pan to prevent it burning.

Place a serving dish over the frying pan and invert to turn out the hoşmerim. When it has cooled sufficiently, pour the honey over it and cover with kaymak. Serve warm, before the kaymak melts.

◊ PEYNIR TATLISI ◊

CHEESE DESSERT

TO SERVE 10
100g/3½oz plain flour
75g/3oz fresh unsalted white cheese, crumbled
50g/2oz butter, cut into small pieces
25g/1oz icing sugar
1 egg
¼tsp bicarbonate of soda
FOR THE SYRUP
250g/8oz caster sugar
250ml/8fl oz water
¼tsp lemon juice
ACCOMPANIMENT
kaymak (p.173) or clotted cream

Sift the flour into a bowl, make a hollow in the centre and add the remaining ingredients. Knead to a dough soft enough to stick to your hand. Place spoonfuls of dough at intervals in a greased large shallow pan or use a pastry bag with a fluted nozzle to squeeze strips 3.5cm/1½ inches apart. Bake in the oven at 200°C/400°F/gas mark 6 for 20 minutes until golden brown.

Meanwhile, make the syrup. Put the water, sugar and lemon juice in a pan on the heat and stir until the sugar melts. Bring to the boil, boil for 2 minutes, then remove from the heat.

Brush the cooked dough with boiling water as soon as the pan is removed from the oven. Cover and leave for 2 minutes, then pour the boiling syrup over the tatlısı and cover. Place over low heat and allow to soak up the syrup for about 5 minutes, from time to time basting with syrup from the pan. Remove from the heat and leave to cool in the pan.

Transfer the tatlısı to a serving dish with a palette knife, taking care not to break them, spread kaymak over the top and serve.

◊ UN HELVASI ◊

FLOUR HELVA

Helvas are the oldest desserts in Turkish cuisine; there is a recipe that dates back to the 11th century.

Like baklava, helva is a traditional dessert frequently served on formal occasions. It is prepared to celebrate the birth of a child; when someone dies helva is served to mourn the loss and is distributed at the graveside. Thus the beginning and end of life are marked with the same dish.

TO SERVE 6
150g/5oz butter
50g/2oz pine nuts
150g/5oz flour
225g/7¹/₂oz caster sugar
400ml/14fl oz water

Melt the butter in a heavy pan. Add the pine nuts and flour and cook on very low heat, stirring, until golden. This may take as long as 40–50 minutes, but it is worth it for good helva.

Boil the sugar and water for 2 minutes to make a syrup. Pour it over the flour, stirring briskly, until it begins to stick to the pan. Remove from the heat. Cover and leave to stand for 15 minutes. Place on a serving dish and serve warm.

◊ KALBURA BASTI ◊
CURLY PASTRY IN SYRUP

TO SERVE 6
75ml/3fl oz milk
75ml/3fl oz olive oil
¼tsp bicarbonate of soda
150g/6oz plain flour
FOR THE SYRUP
150g/6oz caster sugar
125ml/4fl oz water
½tsp lemon juice

Oil a shallow square or oblong pan. Beat the milk, olive oil and bicarbonate of soda in a bowl, add the flour and knead to a smooth dough. Divide into 12 pieces. Take each piece, and with your fingertips press it against a coarse-meshed sieve in a rolling movement to make it curl over. Put the curls in the pan and bake in a preheated oven at 200°C/400°F/gas mark 6 for 20 minutes.

Meanwhile, prepare the syrup by heating together the sugar, water and lemon juice. Boil for 2 minutes, then remove from the heat.

Pour the hot syrup over the pastries as soon as you remove them from the oven. Cover and leave to rest for 10 minutes, then turn and soak the other side in the syrup for 10 minutes. Turn them the right way up and leave until cool.

◊ KAYGANA ◊
KAYGANA FRITTERS

Kaygana is like an unleavened version of lokma, and the yoghurt added to its filling gives it a different taste. The recipe below is from Konya.

TO SERVE 6–8
100g/3½oz thick yoghurt
2 eggs
100g/4oz strong plain flour
¼ tsp bicarbonate of soda
olive or sunflower oil for deep-frying
FOR THE SYRUP
1 quantity of syrup for lokmas (p.139)

Prepare the syrup.

Whisk the yoghurt and eggs together thoroughly. Add the flour and bicarbonate of soda and beat in with a wooden spoon.

Heat the oil. Dip a small spoon into cold oil first, then spoon up some dough, and push it off with your finger into the oil. Repeat until the dough is used up. Fry for 2–3 minutes, turning the kaygana over with a ladle until they are golden. Drain on absorbent paper for a minute, then drop into cold syrup for 3–4 minutes.

Arrange the kaygana on a serving dish, pour over the remaining syrup and serve cold.

◊ IRMIK HELVASI ◊

SEMOLINA HELVA

Semolina helva is a popular dessert for weddings and large parties, and in the old days in Istanbul it was a favourite picnic dish along with cold lamb and dolmas of vine leaves.

The cooking time is rather lengthy but it will ensure a delicious helva. If it is cooked for less than three hours, it will not be as tasty.

TO SERVE 6
150g/5oz butter
50g/2oz pine nuts or almonds
150g/5oz semolina
225g/7½oz caster sugar
400ml/14fl oz milk

Melt the butter in a pan and add the pine nuts or almonds and semolina. Cook on very low heat, stirring constantly with a wooden spoon until golden.

In another pan, heat the sugar and milk, stirring until the sugar melts. Bring to the boil and pour over the semolina mixture, stirring all the time. Cover the pan, and leave on very low heat until all the syrup is absorbed. When holes form on the surface, stir a couple of times, then cover with greaseproof paper and the lid, and lower the heat still further (if necessary use a heat diffuser) and leave for 2 hours.

Stir to break up into grains. Turn on to a heated serving dish and serve hot.

◊ KARA TOPAK HELVA ◊

FUNERAL HELVA

This helva comes from Adıyaman in southeastern Anatolia, where it is traditionally distributed among the mourners three days after a burial. Pekmez, sesame seeds and walnuts give this helva a rich flavour.

TO SERVE 4
75g/3oz butter
100g/3½oz flour
25g/1oz sesame seeds
75ml/3fl oz pekmez (grape syrup p.173)
25g/1oz walnuts, chopped

Melt 50g/2oz of the butter in a frying pan, add the flour and the sesame seeds. Stir for 10 minutes over a very low heat until the flour and seeds are pale yellow in colour but do not let them turn golden. Remove from the heat.

Dilute the pekmez with 50ml/2fl oz water, put in a pan with the remaining butter, and bring to the boil. Remove from the heat and pour over the sesame and flour mixture, stirring briskly. Stir in the walnuts. Allow to cool to lukewarm, then knead by hand as you would a dough. When all the ingredients adhere firmly, roll into balls, place on a serving dish and serve warm.

◊ NIŞASTA HELVASI ◊

WHEATSTARCH HELVA

Nişasta helva is made with pekmez – grape syrup – and has a distinctive flavour.

TO SERVE 4
150ml/¼ pint pekmez (p.173)
150ml/¼ pint water
75–100g/3–3½oz wheat starch (p.173)
75g/3oz butter

Dilute the pekmez (grape syrup) with the water. Put the wheat starch in a bowl. Pour the pekmez into it little by little, stirring constantly until all starchy lumps disappear.

Heat the butter in a frying pan. Pour in the wheat starch and pekmez mixture, stirring briskly. Cook on medium heat, still stirring, until it becomes granulated. It should form granules like bulgur; if it doesn't, put it through a sieve.

Turn on to a serving dish and serve warm.

◊ SÜTLAÇ ◊

RICE PUDDING

In southeastern Anatolia the approach of summer is celebrated at the Festival of Hıdırellez on 6 May, 40 days after the spring equinox, by dressing in white and eating white food, such as milk dishes, rice pudding, pilafs and sarmas of cabbage leaves, to ensure – according to local folklore – that the year ahead be bright in all respects.

TO SERVE 6
75g/3oz rice
1L/1¾ pints milk
pinch of salt
100g/3½oz caster sugar
½tsp cornflour

Soak the rice for 8 hours, then wash until the water runs clear, and strain.

Reserving 1tbsp of milk, boil the rest in a saucepan and allow to cool. Add the rice to the warm milk and place on the heat. Sprinkle with the salt. When it comes to the boil turn the heat to very low and cook for 30–40 minutes until the rice is tender. If it is cooked too quickly, the milk will boil and evaporate and the rice will remain uncooked. Add one third of the sugar and boil for 2 minutes, then another third and boil again for 2 minutes, and finally the remaining third and boil for 5 minutes.

Blend the cornflour with the reserved milk, add to the rice pudding and stir to thicken. Pour into individual bowls and serve cold.

NOTE: If you wish to prepare a richer rice pudding, whisk 1 egg yolk with a pinch of vanilla. Add to it one ladleful of the cooked rice pudding, mix well, then return it to the pudding in the pan. Pour into small bowls, and place under the grill until the surface becomes golden brown.

◊ MUHALLEBI ◊

MILK AND GROUND RICE PUDDING

To prepare sakızlı – a chewy variety of muhallebi – add a mixture of 3 pieces of mastic (p.173) crushed with 1tsp of caster sugar to the muhallebi when it comes to the boil.

TO SERVE 6
1L/1¾ pints milk
75g/3oz sübye (p.173) or 50g/2oz ground rice
150g/5oz caster sugar
1tsp ground cinnamon (optional)

Boil the milk and allow it to cool a little. Stir in the sübye or ground rice and sugar and cook for about 30 minutes on a very low heat, stirring continuously until it thickens.

Pour into individual bowls, allow to stand until cold, then sprinkle with cinnamon.

◊ KEŞKÜL ◊

ALMOND DESSERT

TO SERVE 6–8
75g/3oz sübye (p.173) or 50g/2oz ground rice
1.5L/2½ pints milk
50g/2oz blanched almonds
200g/7oz caster sugar
50g/2oz desiccated coconut
2 egg yolks
25g/1oz pistachio nuts

Boil the milk and leave to cool.

Put the almonds in a blender or food processor, add a cup of the milk and blend until the almonds are pulverized. Add the almond mixture, sugar, half the coconut and the sübye or ground rice to the milk in the pan, and heat gently, stirring. When it comes to the boil turn the heat very low and simmer for 30 minutes, stirring constantly, until it thickens. Then lower the heat and the longer the keşkül simmers the better.

Whisk the eggs in a bowl, then beat in a ladleful of the keşkül. Return the egg mixture to the pan, and simmer for 3 minutes. Do not let it boil.

Pour the keşkül into individual bowls and leave to cool. Boil the pistachio nuts for 1 minute in enough water to cover, remove the skins and dry. Chop them finely.

Garnish the keşkül with the pistachios and the remaining coconut and serve.

◊ TAVUK GÖĞSÜ KAZANDIBI ◊

CHICKEN BREAST DESSERT

Tavuk göğsü is a celebrated Istanbul dessert. In Turkey this is a dish you would buy from a muhallebici – a milk pudding shop; few people would make it at home. It does not taste of chicken at all; it is a delicious, creamy dessert.

The chicken breast must be shredded into thin fibres, which is very time-consuming, and it is said in Turkey that the breast must be taken from a freshly slaughtered chicken if the fibres are to be fine enough.

TO SERVE 6—8
200g/7oz sübye (p.173) or 125g/4oz ground rice
1 small breast of chicken
1L/1¾ pints milk
200g/7oz caster sugar

Put the chicken in a pan with water to cover and simmer until tender. Transfer to a bowl of cold water. Drain and pat dry, then cut lengthways. Hold the ends of the strips with your fingers and rub until they separate into fibres. Continue rubbing towards the middle and separate into fine shreds. Put into cold water and set aside.

Heat the milk gently, and when it comes to the boil stir in the sübye or ground rice. Simmer for 15 minutes, stirring all the time. Add the sugar and cook for a further 10 minutes, still stirring. Then add the chicken breast and cook for another 10 minutes.

Heat a heavy frying pan and pour the tavuk göğsü into it. Brown the underside carefully, shaking the pan. When cool cut into rectangles and serve.

◊ GÜLLAÇ ◊

WAFERS FILLED WITH NUTS

This is a light dessert, much favoured after a heavy evening meal during the month of Ramadan. In the well-to-do homes of old Istanbul, there were always several cooks who specialized in certain types of cooking, such as roasting meat, making börek or desserts, or vegetable dishes. However, when it came to preparing güllaç, this was considered to be the preserve of the lady of the house, for it needs nimble fingers. Güllaç was enjoyed all the more, knowing that the lady of the house had prepared it herself.

TO SERVE 6
150g/5oz shelled walnuts or almonds or coconut
6 sheets of güllaç (ready made starch wafers)
1L/1¾ pints milk
300g/10oz powdered sugar
3tsp rosewater (optional)

Pound the nuts in a mortar or put them through a mincer or food processor. Cut off the hard edges of the güllaç and divide them in half. Boil the milk with the sugar, then remove from the heat.

Place one sheet of güllaç in a shallow pan and pour a ladleful of the milk over it. When the güllaç is soft fold it over three times. Put the soft güllaç in a small coffee cup, press down the middle and spoon in the nut filling, fold the overhanging edges over the filling to meet in the middle and press gently. Prepare all the sheets of gül-laç in the same way and place them on a shallow cooking dish. Pour the remainder of the milk over the güllaç. Cover and bring to the boil over very low heat, then remove from the heat and leave to cool. Sprinkle with rosewater and serve in the dish or in pairs on plates.

NOTE: The güllaç must be eaten without delay, or they will absorb the milk. If serving is delayed pour more sweetened milk over the güllaç before serving.

◊ ZERDE ◊

RICE FLAVOURED WITH SAFFRON

A traditional dessert common in Istanbul and throughout Anatolia. Saffron is expensive and so zerde is served to mark special occasions, such as weddings. A dome-shaped pilaf for a wedding feast is piled on a large copper dish and topped with zerde. No-one can imagine a wedding pilaf without it.

TO SERVE 4–6
½tsp saffron threads
1tbsp rosewater
50g/2oz rice
250ml/8fl oz water
150g/5oz caster sugar
1tsp wheat starch or cornflour
2tbsp warm water
25g/1oz pine nuts
1tsp cinnamon
seeds of half a pomegranate
25g/1oz currants

Soak the saffron in the rosewater overnight.

Pick over and wash the rice. Cook in the water over very low heat for 25–30 minutes until the rice is tender. Add the sugar in three stages, as in the previous recipe, to prevent the rice remaining hard. Mix in the rosewater flavoured with saffron. When it comes to the boil, blend the wheat starch with warm water and slowly add to the zerde while stirring. Cook for 5 minutes.

Ladle the zerde into individual bowls. Toast the pine nuts in a dry frying pan until golden. When the zerde has cooled, garnish with pine nuts, cinnamon, pomegranate seeds and currants. Serve cold.

◊ PALUZE ◊
BLANCMANGE

This is an Anatolian dessert traditionally given to new mothers to help them to breast-feed their newborn baby.

TO SERVE 6–8
50g/2oz caster sugar
50g/2oz wheat starch or cornflour
1tbsp rosewater
25g/1oz chopped pistachio nuts or walnuts or blanched almonds
1tsp cinnamon

Bring 1L/1¾ pints of water and the sugar to the boil. Whisk the wheat starch into 100ml/3½fl oz cold water. When the syrup begins to boil, stir in the wheat starch mixture. Keep stirring over very low heat until the mixture becomes translucent and thickens, at which point add the rosewater. Cook for another minute then pour into small bowls.

While still hot garnish with pistachio nuts. Allow to cool and serve sprinkled with cinnamon.

◊ KESME BULAMACI ◊
SPICED BULGUR PUDDING

This dessert is a speciality of the South East. It is rather thick and is served as a snack during the winter.

TO SERVE 4–6
50g/2oz finely ground bulgur
150ml/¼ pint pekmez (grape syrup p.173)
small piece cinnamon
1 allspice berry
5 cloves
1tsp wheat starch or cornflour
1tsp flour
25g/1oz sesame seeds
25g/1oz walnuts, crushed

Cook the bulgur in 500ml/17fl oz of water until tender – about 10 minutes. There should be 450ml/¾ pint liquid left in the pan; top up with boiling water if necessary. Add the pekmez and the spices tied in a piece of muslin. Cover the pan and when it comes to the boil, turn the heat very low and simmer for 15 minutes, stirring occasionally. Blend the wheat starch and flour with 50ml/2fl oz water in a bowl, and stir into the bulamaç. Roast the sesame seeds in a dry pan until golden and add to the bulamaç with the crushed walnuts. Cook, uncovered, for a further 5–10 minutes, stirring occasionally until the bulamaç thickens, then remove from the heat. Discard the bag of spices and serve cold in individual bowls.

◊ SALEPLI DONDURMA ◊

SALEP ICE CREAM

This Turkish ice cream has a delicate and unusual flavour. Sometimes mastic (p.173) is added, which gives it a special taste.

TO SERVE 6
500ml/17fl oz milk
50g/2oz caster sugar
1tsp salep (p.168)
FOR THE GARNISH
bitter chocolate

Prepare the salep mixture as described on p.168. Remove from the heat and cool, then transfer to an aluminium or pyrex bowl and place in the freezer or freeze in an ice cream machine according to the manufacturer's instructions.

Freeze, stirring occasionally with a wooden spoon.

Serve in individual bowls garnished with grated bitter chocolate.

◊ VİŞNELİ EKMEK TATLISI ◊
BREAD AND MORELLO CHERRY
DESSERT

TO SERVE 6
125g/4oz stale white bread
125g/4oz butter
250g/8oz morello cherries, stoned
200ml/7fl oz water
200g/7oz caster sugar
ACCOMPANIMENT
kaymak (p.173), clotted or double cream

Slice the bread and toast lightly. Heat the butter in a frying pan and fry the toast for 2–3 minutes until golden. Drain on absorbent paper then arrange the slices in a shallow flameproof casserole.

Put the cherries and water in another pan, bring to the boil, add the sugar and stir. Simmer very gently, uncovered, for 10 minutes, then pour over the bread. Cover and simmer for another 5 minutes on very low heat. Remove from the heat and allow to cool in the pan.

Spread with kaymak, clotted or whisked double cream and serve cold.

◊ AŞURE ◊
DESSERT WITH CEREALS,
DRIED FRUITS AND NUTS

Aşure is a feast day observed on the 10th of Muharram (the first month of the Moslem calendar) to mark Noah's salvation from the flood. Noah is said to have cooked aşure from the foodstuffs remaining in the ark when the flood subsided. It also marks the martyrdom of the Prophet's grandsons Hasan and Hüseyin on that day.

TO SERVE 8—10
100g/3½oz döğme (p.119)
2L/3½ pints water
20g/¾oz chickpeas
20g/¾oz haricot beans
20g/¾oz dried broad beans
50g/2oz rice
20g/¾oz sultanas
20g/¾oz dried figs
20g/¾oz dried apricots

1tbsp wheat starch or cornflour
100ml/3½fl oz milk
25g/1oz butter
200g/7oz caster sugar
25g/1oz hazelnuts
100ml/3½fl oz rosewater
50g/2oz shelled walnuts
2tbsp pomegranate seeds
1tsp sesame seeds
1tsp ground cinnamon
1tsp nigella (p.173)

Pick over and wash the döğme. Put it in a pan with the water, bring to the boil, take off the heat and leave to soak overnight. Soak the chickpeas, haricot beans and broad beans separately overnight, too, then cook separately in fresh water until tender. Rub the peas and beans to slip off the skins. Soak the rice in water, also overnight, wash in the morning and drain.

Put the sultanas, figs and apricots in separate small pans, cover with water and cook for 10 minutes, then drain and chop the last two as small as the hazelnuts.

Blend the wheat starch thoroughly with the milk.

Cook the döğme in its own liquid (if reduced top up to 2L/3½ pints) for about 1 hour or until tender. Then add the rice, dried fruits and butter. Once it comes to the boil add the chickpeas, haricots and broad beans. Cook on medium heat for 10 minutes until all the ingredients are soft. Then add the sugar at four intervals as the aşure boils, a quarter at a time. (If the sugar is added all at once, the wheat will harden.)

Add the hazelnuts. Cook for 15 minutes, stirring continuously, or until the aşure thickens. It is essential to stir after adding the sugar or the aşure will burn and stick to the bottom of the pan. Add the milk and wheat starch, bring to the boil, pour in the rosewater and remove from the heat.

Pour the aşure into a serving dish or into small individual bowls.

Toast the walnuts in a dry frying pan, then chop them and sprinkle over the aşure together with the pomegranate seeds, sesame seeds, cinnamon and nigella. Serve hot or cold.

◊ AYVA TATLISI ◊
QUINCE DESSERT

TO SERVE 6
500g/1lb medium sized quinces
150g/5fl oz water
200g/7oz caster sugar
100g/3½oz kaymak (p.173) or clotted cream

Peel the quinces and cut them in half, removing the seeds and core. Put in a pan with the water, cover and parboil over low heat for about 5 minutes. Strain the quinces, reserving the liquid. Add the sugar to the liquid and boil for 1 minute, then remove from the heat.

Return the quinces to the pan, cover, and cook over very low heat until the quinces are tender, spooning the syrup over them from time to time until it is absorbed. Cool in the pan.

Place on a serving dish, fill the centres with kaymak and serve cold.

◊ KAYISI TATLISI ◊

A P R I C O T   D E S S E R T

TO SERVE 4
125g/4oz dried sour apricots (avoid sweet fruit)
75g/3oz caster sugar
100g/3½oz kaymak (p.173) or clotted cream
50g/2oz blanched almonds

Soak the apricots in water overnight. Strain and cook in 500ml/17fl oz water until tender – about 10 minutes. Strain, retaining the liquid.

Put 75ml/3fl oz of the liquid into a pan and add the sugar, bring to the boil and boil for 1 minute then pour over the apricots. Cook the apricots over very low heat for 20–25 minutes. Cool in the pan.

Open up each apricot and fill with kaymak and an almond. Place on a serving dish and garnish with the remaining almonds. Serve cold.

◊ ÜZÜM VE KAYISI HOŞAFI ◊

S U L T A N A   A N D   A P R I C O T   C O M P O T E

Stewed fruit desserts and compotes using the enormous variety of local produce are very popular in Anatolia.

In Turkish popular cuisine stewed fruit is called "the final say"; everyone knows that when stewed fruit is served there will be no more dishes to follow.

TO SERVE 4–6
100g/3½oz sultanas
50g/2oz dried apricots
1L/1¾ pints water
200g/7oz caster sugar

Soak the sultanas and dried apricots overnight. Strain and transfer to a pan with the water. When it comes to the boil, reduce the heat and cook for 10 minutes. Add the sugar and cook for another 10 minutes, then remove from the heat and cool in the pan. Transfer to a serving dish or individual bowls, and serve cold.

◊ BAL KABAĞI TATLISI ◊

PUMPKIN DESSERT

In Antalya legend has it that the Prophet Mohammed ate pumpkin before ascending to heaven and so this dessert is made and distributed on Mirac, his Ascension Day.

TO SERVE 4–6
1kg/2lb pumpkin
150g/5oz sugar
25ml/1fl oz water
2 cloves
100g/3½oz walnuts, chopped

Cut the pumpkin into 2.5cm/1 inch cubes and place in a shallow pan. Sprinkle with sugar, add the water and cloves and cover.

Cook on very low heat for about 30 minutes until tender. Cool in the pan.

Place in a serving dish and garnish with the walnuts.

◊ BADEM EZMESI ◊

ALMOND MARZIPAN

250g/8oz shelled almonds
50g/2oz pistachio nuts
250g/8oz icing sugar
¼tsp vanilla essence
25ml/1fl oz (approx.) rosewater

It is important to use new crop almonds, not more than three months after harvesting.

Blanch and dry the pistachio nuts and almonds. Finely chop the pistachios. Pound or process the almonds into a paste with the sugar and vanilla essence. Mix the paste with enough rosewater to make it adhere well and knead for 10–15 minutes. Roll out into a long stick. Cut it up into small pieces or roll into small balls in the palm of the hand. Coat with chopped pistachio nuts. Leave in the refrigerator for 2–3 hours before serving.

◊ SADE LOKUM ◊

TURKISH DELIGHT

Lokum is one of the most famous Turkish sweets. In addition to plain lokum, known as lati lokum, there is a great variety of lokums known by the methods of preparation or by the name of the ingredients. Çifte kavrulmu – twice-cooked – lokum and fındıkl – hazelnut – lokum, are a couple of examples.

Hazel and pistachio nut lokum are prepared by skinning the nuts and dry roasting them for 5–10 minutes in the oven before adding them to the cooked lokum just as it is removed from the heat.

Sakızlı – chewy – lokum is made by adding crushed mastic to the lokum at the end of the cooking time.

Lokum is left to set in moulds dusted with wheat starch, or occasionally with grated coconut. Good lokum will keep for six months to a year in a dry atmosphere. Lokum is usually made industrially, but it is possible to make smaller quantities at home.

TO MAKE 1–1.5KG/2–3LBS
1kg/2lb caster sugar
225g/7oz cornflour (Çorlu brand)
1.2L/2 pints water
¼tsp lemon salt crystals (not lumps)
100g/3½oz icing sugar
25–30cm/10–12 inch square tin
35cm/12 inch square of nylon or muslin

Line the tin with nylon or muslin and dust thickly with half the cornflour.

Place the caster sugar, remaining cornflour and water in a large preserving pan. Stir thoroughly with a long-handled wooden spoon and bring to the boil over high heat. Add the lemon salt and boil, stirring continuously. When the mixture starts to foam and rise lower the heat a little. Stir continuously until the mixture reaches the soft ball stage (112°–116°C/234°–240°F on a sugar thermometer). The lokum can occasionally "spit" and burn the hand, so wear an old pair of gloves. To determine whether the consistency is right, remove the pan from the heat and drop a little of the mixture, which should no longer stick to the pan, into a bowl of iced water. Under the water form it into a ball with your fingers, then lift it out. If it is pliable and starts to flatten between your fingers, it is ready.

Pour the lokum into the mould and leave to set. Spread icing sugar on a marble slab. Turn the lokum on to a tray. Remove the cloth, brush off the cornflour and put the lokum on the icing sugar. Dip a sharp knife in icing sugar and cut the lokum into squares. Coat all over with icing sugar and transfer to a box or a sweet dish.

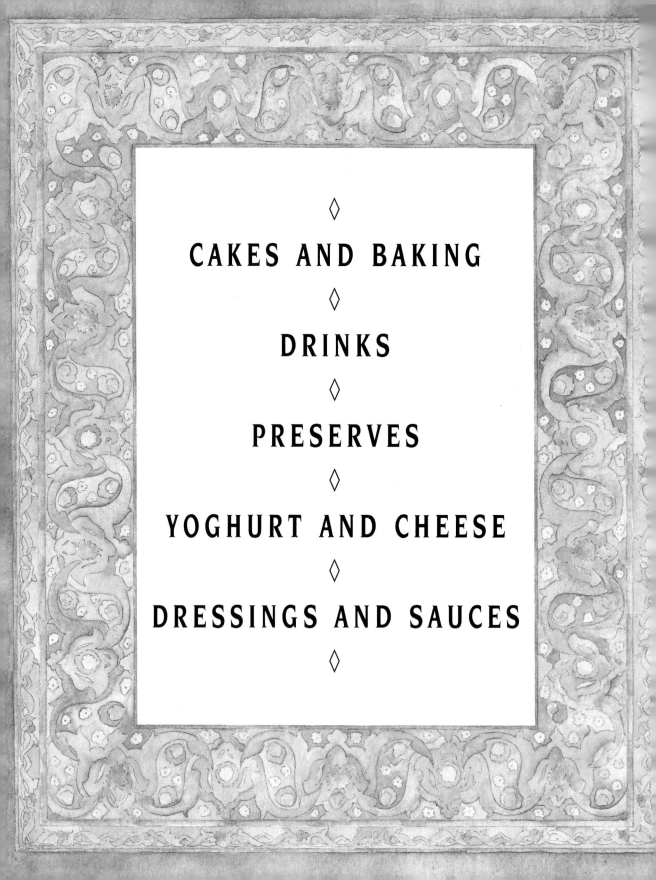

◊

CAKES AND BAKING

◊

DRINKS

◊

PRESERVES

◊

YOGHURT AND CHEESE

◊

DRESSINGS AND SAUCES

◊

◊ KREMALI PASTA ◊

CREAM SPONGE

TO SERVE 16
FOR THE FILLING
200ml/7fl oz milk
1 egg
50g/2oz caster sugar
½tsp lemon zest
½tsp orange zest
30g/1¼oz plain flour
a few drops of vanilla essence
½tsp butter
TO SOAK SPONGE
100ml/3½fl oz milk
FOR THE ICING
500ml/¾ pint milk
50g/2oz caster sugar
50g/2oz cornflour
300g/10oz butter
FOR THE SPONGE
175g/6¼oz flour
a few drops of vanilla essence
1tsp lemon zest
6 eggs
175g/6¼oz sugar
30cm/12 inch round cake tin

Grease the cake tin with a little butter and sprinkle with 1tbsp of flour. Tap the tin, and turn it to coat all sides.

Boil the milk for the filling and put to one side. Whisk the egg, sugar, lemon and orange zest in a pan, put it on very low heat, and warm through, whisking all the time. Remove from the heat and stir in the flour. Return to very low heat and whisk in the hot milk. When it begins to boil and thicken remove from the heat and add the vanilla and butter. Do not stir too briskly now. As the mixture cools, stir occasionally to prevent the filling from hardening or cover with greaseproof paper. It should stay creamy. Boil the milk for soaking the sponge, let it cool and remove the skin.

To prepare the icing boil half the milk with the sugar in an enamel pan. Blend the remainder with the cornflour and whisk into the boiling milk. When it becomes jelly-like and thickens remove it from the heat and leave to cool, stirring occasionally.

Cream the butter thoroughly then beat in the cold cornflour, a spoonful at a time, to obtain a smooth creamy consistency.

To prepare the sponge: sift the flour into a bowl and add the vanilla and lemon zest. Cream the eggs and sugar and fold in the flour. Fill the cake tin and bake for 30–35 minutes in a preheated oven at 175°C/350°F/gas mark 4. It is ready when a skewer inserted in the middle comes out clean. Cool on a rack, then cut the sponge in half with a very sharp knife. Put both halves, cut side uppermost, on the rack and brush with milk. Let it soak in and leave for 3 hours.

Then spread the filling on one half and cover with the other; it is often better to use the bottom half of the sponge to make the top. With a spatula cover the sponge all over with half of the icing and transfer it to the serving plate. Put the remainder of the icing in a piping bag and decorate the top of the sponge. Chill for 2–3 hours on the bottom shelf of the refrigerator before serving.

◊ CEVIZLI AY ◊
WALNUT CRESCENTS

TO MAKE 12 CRESCENT-SHAPED BUNS
FOR THE FILLING
50ml/2fl oz milk
100g/3½oz walnuts, finely chopped
25g/1oz sultanas
25g/1oz dry breadcrumbs
½tsp cinnamon
½tsp allspice
½tsp vanilla essence
1tsp lemon zest
100g/3½oz caster sugar
FOR THE DOUGH
250g/8oz strong plain flour
½tsp dried yeast
4tbsp warm milk
½tsp caster sugar
150g/5oz butter
1 egg yolk
FOR THE GLAZE
1tsp icing sugar
1 egg

Grease a baking tray, then prepare the filling. Heat the milk and add the walnuts and when it comes to the boil lower the heat and cook, stirring, for 3–4 minutes. Remove the pan from the heat and add the sultanas then the breadcrumbs, spices and lemon zest. Mix well, then stir in the sugar and leave to cool.

To prepare the dough put the yeast to prove with the warm milk and sugar. Sift the flour into a bowl, make a well in the middle and add the yeast mixture when it becomes frothy. Draw in the flour from the sides and mix thoroughly. Cover and leave to rise in a warm place. When it has almost doubled in bulk punch it down and knead in the butter and egg. Divide into 12 pieces. Leave on a wooden board sprinkled with flour and covered with a damp cloth for 20 minutes in a cool place.

Flour the work surface and roll out the pieces of dough into oval shapes 5mm/¼ inch thick. Spread the cold filling on the dough and roll like cigarettes. Curve the ends round to form a crescent shape. Place them on the baking tray, cover, and leave for 30 minutes to rise again, this time in a warm place.

Make a glaze with the icing sugar and egg. Brush the mixture over the crescents and bake in a preheated oven at 200°C/400°F/gas mark 6 for 20–25 minutes.

◊ KÜLÜNCE ◊
SPICE CAKES

In Şanlı Urfa in southeastern Anatolia, it is customary for a young man about to leave to do his military service to be given a külünce from which he takes a small bite. The külünce is then hung on the wall as a good omen for his safe return. When he completes his military service and eventually returns, he has the customary egg cooked over a fire made of his letters home (p.44) and then he breaks off a small piece from the külünce and eats it; the rest is soaked in water, crumbled and put out into the garden or yard for the birds.

If the külünce is being cooked for a

departing young recruit, a hole is made in the middle before baking so that it can be hung up.

TO MAKE 4 KÜLÜNCE
300g/10oz strong plain flour
½tsp dried yeast
25ml/1fl oz milk
75g/3oz caster sugar
50g/2oz melted butter
25ml/1fl oz olive oil
75ml/3fl oz milk or water
1 egg
¼tsp cinnamon
¼tsp çemen (see NOTE) or fenugreek
¼tsp dried coconut
¼tsp mahleb (optional, see NOTE)
¼tsp ground cloves
¼tsp ground liquorice
1 egg yolk

Grease a baking tray. Prove the yeast in warm milk with ¼tsp of the sugar. Sift the flour into a bowl and make a well in the middle. When the yeast mixture has frothed up pour it into the well and draw in the flour.

Mix to a dough, cover and leave to rise. Knock back gently, hollow out the centre and add the melted butter, olive oil, milk, egg, remaining sugar and spices. Knead to a firm dough.

Divide the dough into four pieces. Roll out to 2.5cm/1 inch thickness and transfer to the baking tray. Cover and leave to rise in a warm place for 1 hour.

Mix the egg yolk with a few drops of water and brush the tops of the külünce. Bake in a preheated oven at 200°C/400°F/ gas mark 6 for 20–25 minutes. Serve hot or cold.

NOTE: Çemen is a spice blend used to coat pastırma. It is made by mixing ground fenugreek, crushed garlic and paprika with a little salt and enough water to make a paste.

Mahleb is the fruit of a wild plum, dried and used for flavouring.

◊ YOĞURTLU KEK ◊
YOGHURT CAKE

TO SERVE 10
300g/10oz self-raising flour
½tsp baking powder
250g/8oz butter
250g/8oz plain yoghurt
¼tsp vanilla essence
250g/8oz caster sugar
3 eggs
35cm/14 inch cake tin

Grease the tin and set it aside.
Sift the flour and baking powder together.

Melt the butter, pour it into a bowl and stir in the yoghurt and vanilla.

In another bowl whisk the sugar and eggs until creamy then pour in the yoghurt mixture, mixing well with a large spoon. Fold in the flour and turn the mixture into the cake tin.

Bake in a preheated oven at 200°C/400°F/ gas mark 6 for 20–25 minutes until the surface is golden brown.

Cool in the tin until bearable to the touch then turn out on to a wire rack. When cold cut into square or diamond shapes.

◊ UN KURABIYESI ◊

PLAIN SWEET BISCUITS

Un kurabiyesi literally means "made with flour". It is one of the oldest biscuits.

24 KURABIYE
100g/3½oz butter or margarine
50g/2oz sugar
175g/6oz plain flour
24 cloves
icing sugar

Cream the butter and sugar and then work in the flour to form a smooth dough.

Divide the dough in two. Shape each piece into a long cylinder and cut into 12 slices. Lightly press down with the palm on each slice. Alternatively, cut the dough into 24 pieces and roll in the palm of the hand into balls. Press the middle down with the finger and stick a clove into each one. Place in rows on a greased baking tray and bake for 15 minutes in a preheated oven at 150°C/300°F/gas mark 2, taking care not to allow the surface to become too brown.

Put some icing sugar in a bowl and dip both sides of the kurabiye in it before serving.

◊ KANDIL SIMIDI ◊

KANDIL ROLLS

These simits, baked during the Kandil religious feast days (see p.17), have a special flavour that comes from mahleb. On Kandil days the air outside bakeries and patisseries is filled with the smell of kandil simits, creating a special festive atmosphere. Kandil simidi goes well with salep (p.168).

TO MAKE 16 SIMITS
150g/5oz strong plain flour
2tbsp milk
½tsp dry yeast
2tbsp milk
¼tsp caster sugar
75g/3oz butter
1 egg
½tsp mahleb (p.161)
½tsp salt
1–2 egg yolks
25g/1oz sesame seeds

Put the warm milk, yeast and sugar in a small bowl and leave to prove. Sift the flour into a bowl, make a hollow in the middle and add the frothy yeast mixture. Draw the flour from the sides and mix to a dough. Leave to rise, then knock back and add the butter, egg, mahleb and salt. Knead to a smooth dough. Cover and leave to rise in a warm place for 1 hour.

Divide the dough into 16 pieces. Roll on a board or in the hands into a long roll, then join the ends to make a circle. Mix the egg yolk with a little water, dip the simits first in this mixture, and then into sesame seeds. Put them on a greased baking tray 1cm/½ inch apart.

Bake in a preheated oven at 200°C/400°F/ gas mark 6 for 20 minutes.

◊ YOĞURTLU POĞAÇA ◊
SAVOURY PASTRY WITH YOGHURT

This poğaça is mostly made at home.

TO MAKE 30 POĞAÇAS
300g/10oz plain flour
½tsp bicarbonate of soda
1tsp salt
100g/3½oz butter
100g/3½oz yoghurt
1 egg plus 1 yolk
½ quantity cheese or minced meat filling for börek (p.130)

Sift the flour into a bowl with the bicarbonate of soda and salt. Make a well in the middle and put in the butter, yoghurt and egg and blend. Draw in the flour from the sides and mix to a soft dough. Rest for 15 minutes covered, under a well wrung-out cloth. Take a small piece of dough, flatten it out between the palms of the hands, put in a little of the filling and fold over the edges. Seal. Turn over so the join is underneath and put the poğaças on a greased baking sheet. Repeat with the rest of the dough; there should be enough for about 30 poğaças.

Beat the egg yolk with a few drops of water and glaze the pastries, then bake in a preheated oven at 200°C/400°F/gas mark 6 for 20–25 minutes.

◊ BIRA MAYALI POĞAÇA ◊
CHEESE PASTRIES

Poğaças are made at home and at pastry shops and eaten, hot or cold, for breakfast or as a snack.

TO MAKE 20 POĞAÇAS
275g/9oz flour
1tsp dried yeast
25ml/1fl oz warm milk
½tsp caster sugar
150ml/¼ pint milk
125g/4oz butter
1 egg
1tsp salt
1 quantity cheese filling for börek (p.130)
1 egg yolk

Prove the yeast in warm milk, with the sugar. Sift the flour into a bowl, hollow out the middle and pour in the yeast mixture when it froths. Draw in the flour from the sides, blend, and mix to a dough. Cover and leave to rise. Punch down, hollow out the middle and add the butter, egg and salt. Knead to a soft dough (as soft as an ear lobe) and divide into 20 pieces. Cover and leave in a warm place for 30 minutes.

Take each piece of dough and flatten it between the palms of the hands. Put some of the filling on one side of each circle of dough, fold over and seal the edges firmly. Put the pastries on a greased baking sheet, uncovered, and in a warm place for 30 minutes. Beat the egg yolk with a few drops of water and glaze the tops before baking in a preheated oven at 200°C/400°F/gas mark 6 for 20–25 minutes.

◊ ÇÖREK ◊
S A V O U R Y   B I S C U I T S

TO SERVE 8–10
200g/7oz strong plain flour
½tsp dried yeast
¼tsp caster sugar
25ml/1fl oz warm milk
¼tsp cinnamon
¼tsp çemen (p.161) or fenugreek
¼tsp dried coconut
¼tsp mahleb (p.161)
¼tsp ground cloves
¼tsp ground liquorice
½tsp salt
50g/2oz melted butter
75ml/3fl oz milk or water
1 egg
1–2 egg yolks mixed with a little water
1tsp nigella (p.173)

Prove the yeast with the sugar in the milk. Sift the flour into a bowl, add all the spices, salt and proved yeast mixture. Blend.

Leave to rise, then knock back and work in the melted warm butter, milk or water and egg. Knead to a firm dough. Divide in two, cover and leave to rise for about 1 hour in a warm place.

Roll out the risen dough, sprinkling it with a little flour, to 5mm/¼ inch thick. With a sharp knife cut diagonally (like baklava slices). Prick with a fork and brush with egg glaze, sprinkle with nigella and place on a greased sheet. Leave to rest for 15 minutes in a warm place. Bake in a preheated oven at 200°C/400°F/gas mark 6 for 20–25 minutes.

◊ KAYISI BISKÜVISI ◊
A P R I C O T   B I S C U I T S

TO MAKE 20 BISCUITS
250g/8oz plain flour
125g/4oz butter
2 egg yolks
100g/3½oz icing sugar
¼tsp vanilla essence
½tsp lemon zest
pinch salt
100g/3½oz apricot marmalade
green, yellow and red food colouring
150g/5oz caster sugar
small firm leaves

Sift the flour on to a pastry board. Put the cold butter in the middle and with a knife dice the butter and flour into tiny grains like bulgur. Hollow out the middle like a bowl. Put in the egg yolks. Round the edges sprinkle icing sugar, vanilla, lemon zest and salt. Knead, beginning from the centre and drawing in the sides. If the dough is too hard add more butter, if too soft add more flour. Knead just long enough to make a smooth dough. Cover with a well wrung-out damp cloth and leave to rest for 20 minutes.

Take small lumps of dough, slightly bigger than a hazelnut, and roll in the hand into 40 small balls and place them in rows on a greased baking tray. Bake in a pre-heated oven at 200°C/400°F/gas mark 6 for 15–20 minutes. Cool on the tray.

When cold lift the balls off with a knife. With a pointed knife hollow out the under-sides of the balls, taking care not to break them. Gather up the biscuit crumbs and crush to a powder. Mix 2tbsp with the apricot marmalade.

Wash the leaves and dry them. In three separate bowls mix green, yellow and red colouring with water. Put the caster sugar on a plate.

Fill the hollows in the biscuits with the marmalade and biscuit mixture and stick the biscuits together in pairs. Dip the biscuits quickly into the green, yellow or red colouring, then roll in sugar. Stick the leaves into the biscuits and serve.

All this should be done quickly as the biscuits may crumble.

◊ HAŞHAŞLI ÇÖREK ◊
POPPY-SEED BISCUITS

Haşhaşlı çörek, in some places known as haşhaşlı lokum, is much favoured in the hinterland of the Aegean region. This çörek, which has a different flavour because of the poppy seeds, is served at breakfast and tea and is also taken on picnics.

½tsp dried yeast
¼tsp caster sugar
150ml/¼ pint warm water
250g/8oz strong plain flour
½tsp salt
½ quantity poppy seed filling (p.133)
1 egg yolk mixed with water
20g/1¾oz sesame seeds

Let the yeast prove with the sugar in a little warm water. When it froths, add to the sifted flour and salt and blend to a dough. Leave to rise, then knock back and add the remaining water. Knead to a very soft dough.

Divide in two, cover and leave to rise for about 1 hour in a warm place. Roll out the dough, which will be very sticky, sprinkling flour underneath and on top. Spread the filling over the surface and roll into a tube. Cut with a sharp knife into 5–6cm/2–2½ inch lengths, put them on a greased baking sheet and leave to rest for 10 minutes.

Brush with egg yolk mixture. Dip two fingers in the egg mixture and then in the sesame seeds and press them on to the çörek.

Bake in a preheated oven at 250°C/500°F/gas mark 10 for 20 minutes. When removed from the oven, cover and leave to cool.

◊ IÇKILER ◊
D R I N K S

Both alcoholic and non-alcoholic drinks have a place in Turkish cuisine. The most famous Turkish alcoholic drink is of course the rakı, although beers and a number of table wines are produced. During the Ottoman period alcoholic drinks were periodically banned, but their consumption has continued to the present day.

◊ LIMON ŞERBETI ◊
L E M O N   S H E R B E T

Sherbets are light cooling drinks that used to be served between courses at banquets in order to refresh the appetite. They are made from fresh seasonal fruit or flowers that impart aroma and colour and are now drunk at any time of day.

the rind of 2 lemons, grated
4 mint leaves, 2tbsp sugar
150ml/¼ pint lemon juice

100g/3½oz sugar
600ml/1 pint water

Pound the lemon rind, mint leaves and 2tbsp of the sugar together in a mortar. Tie up the resulting paste in a piece of muslin.

Heat together the lemon juice, remaining sugar and water and stir until the sugar melts. Add the muslin bag and chill for 10–12 hours, then strain through muslin.

◊ GÜL ŞERBETI ◊
S W E E T E N E D   R O S E   S H E R B E T

Rose sherbet is an old favourite, served at many traditional gatherings and ceremonial functions. Elizabeth I's ambassador to the Ottoman Court, Edward Banton, wrote in his report that he had attended a dinner at which one hundred different dishes were served, including sherbet.

Rose sherbet can be prepared with rose water as well as petals by adding enough rosewater or rose essence to impart a scent of roses to 200ml/7fl oz of water and 40g/1½oz of sugar.

100g/3½oz scented rose petals
25ml/1fl oz lemon juice

150g/5oz caster sugar
1L/1¾ pints water

Cut off the white base of the rose petals and put the petals in a bowl. Add the lemon juice and rub well with the hands for 5–10 minutes. Leave to stand for 30 minutes.

Bring the sugar and water to the boil, boil for 1 minute then remove from the heat. Let the syrup cool a little then pour it over the roses. Leave in the refrigerator for 10–12 hours. Strain through muslin and pour into decanters. Pour a little sherbet on to a plate. Dip the rim of a glass into it and then into icing sugar. Allow to dry then fill the glass with cold sherbet and serve.

◊ KAHVE ◊

COFFEE

*"On your way to an Istanbul boulevard
Might there not be a moment to spare?
To talk about the cost of living and so on
And drink our bitter coffee?"*

FEYZI HALICI 'ISTANBUL BOULEVARD'

TO SERVE 1
50ml/2fl oz water (one coffee cupful)
½tsp sugar
½tsp coffee, ground

Coffee has been prepared and served in coffee houses since the 16th century. It is made in a small long-handled pot called a cezve and served in small cups, and a dish of lokum or other sweetmeat is usually offered with it. In the southern part of Anatolia cardamom is sometimes added to coffee to enhance its taste, but real coffee addicts prefer it plain to savour its natural flavour.

Put the water in the pot and stir in the sugar and coffee. Put over low heat and heat until the coffee rises. Remove from the heat and pour the froth from the top into the cup. Return the pot to the heat, bring to the boil and remove from the heat. Repeat twice more, then pour into the cup.

This quantity of sugar makes medium sweet – orta – coffee; sade means coffee without sugar; tatlı means sweet.

◊ ÇAY ◊

TEA

Nowadays tea is drunk even more widely than coffee. It is served plain, in small glasses, with or without sugar.

In Anatolia the "kırtlama" fashion of drinking it is common – a cube of sugar is held in the mouth to sweeten the tea as it is drunk. Kırtlama addicts can drink three or four cups of tea with only one lump of sugar lasting through it all.

TO SERVE 6
6tsp tea
water

Heat water in a large kettle, remove the lid and rest a china teapot on top of the kettle.

When the water boils put the tea in the teapot. Pour some boiling water into it, swirl the tea around and pour off the liquid immediately. Add 200ml/7fl oz boiling water to the teapot and place on top of the kettle. Cover the teapot with a clean cloth to prevent the aroma of tea from escaping.

Turn the heat under the kettle very low. Let the tea brew for 7–10 minutes until tea leaves float to the surface. Pour the tea into glasses before the leaves sink to the bottom of the pot, and serve. For those who like strong tea, fill the cup; for weaker tea, pour in only a little tea and top up with hot water.

◊ BOZA ◊

BULGUR DRINK

Boza is very popular in winter. Street vendors sell boza from copper jugs, calling out: "Sweet and bitter boza!"

150g/5oz bulgur, 25g/1oz rice
3L/5¼ pints water
300g/10oz caster sugar
½tsp yeast, 1tsp cinnamon

Put the bulgur, rice and water in a large pan, cover, and cook for about 1½ hours until reduced to pulp. Sieve, and put the purée back into the pan (there should be about 2½L/4¼ pints of rather liquid purée). Add the sugar and bring to the boil, stirring continuously. After 2 minutes remove from the heat and leave to cool somewhat. While still warm pour into a bowl.

Blend the yeast with a little of the warm liquid and when it rises mix into the boza. Cover and leave at room temperature to ferment. When it has bubbles on the surface – it usually takes about 8 hours – it is ready. It should have a bittersweet taste.

Pour into large boza glasses, sprinkle with cinnamon and serve with leblebi (roasted chickpeas).

◊ SALEP ◊

SALEP

Salep is a hot drink made with the powdered root of the salep orchid – *Orchis mascula*. In the winter, people often have a cup of salep with a couple of simits before rushing off to work in the morning. It is sold from copper urns on street corners and at stations throughout Turkey.

TO SERVE 2–3
500ml/17fl oz milk

½tsp salep
50g/2oz caster sugar
¼tsp ground ginger
¼tsp ground cinnamon

Heat the milk and add the salep with 2tbsp sugar. When it comes to the boil stir in the remaining sugar and simmer for 10 minutes stirring frequently, until it thickens. Serve hot, sprinkled with ginger and cinnamon.

◊ AYRAN ◊

YOGHURT DRINK

Ayran is often drunk with meals. The consistency can be changed by adding more or less water.

TO SERVE 3–4
500g/1lb thick-set yoghurt
400ml/14fl oz iced water
1tsp salt or to taste

Put the yoghurt in a bowl and whisk for 1–2 minutes until smooth. Add the water and salt gradually and whisk again for 2 minutes. Ayran can be made in a blender too.

◊ VIŞNE REÇELI ◊

MORELLO CHERRY JAM

800g/1lb 10oz granulated sugar
400ml/14fl oz water
¼tsp lemon salt (optional)
500g/1lb stoned morello cherries (weight after stoning)

Make a syrup with the sugar, water and lemon salt. When it comes to the boil, reduce the heat and 2 minutes later add the cherries.

Bring back to the boil, remove from the heat and leave to stand for 30 minutes to allow the fruit to absorb the sugar. Then return to the heat and boil for 25–30 minutes or longer, carefully watching the consistency. Test for setting and remove any scum from the surface. Cool and pot in warm jars. Cover when cold.

Cornelian cherry jam is made in the same way but the fruit is not stoned.

◊ AYVA MARMELATI ◊

QUINCE MARMALADE

400g/14oz quinces
600ml/1 pint water
800g/1lb sugar
2tbsp lemon juice

Peel and core the quinces and grate them.

Put the grated quinces in a pan with the water, cover and boil for about 30 minutes, or until tender.

Strain the boiled quinces, retaining the liquid. Top up the liquid to 400ml/14fl oz with hot water if necessary. Add the sugar and lemon juice and boil for 1 minute. Put the quinces into the boiling syrup and boil, uncovered, for 5 minutes. Remove from the heat and leave to stand for 3 hours so that the quince takes on a pinkish colour.

Bring the marmalade to the boil again and cook gently for 20–25 minutes or longer to reach setting point. Pot in warmed jars and cover when cold.

◊ ŞEFTALI MARMELATI ◊

PEACH MARMALADE

Apricot marmalade can be prepared in the same way.

1 quantity jam syrup (above)
600g/1¼lb ripe peaches

Peel the peaches and remove the stones.

Purée the flesh. Boil the syrup for 2 minutes then add the peach purée. Cook on medium heat, stirring occasionally, for 35–40 minutes until setting point is reached. Remove the pan from the heat, skim off any froth and pot the marmalade while still warm. Cover when cold.

◊ KARIŞIK TURŞU ◊
MIXED PICKLES

Turkish cuisine has a wealth of pickles. Every town has at least one specialist pickle shop with jars of pickled fruits and vegetables of every conceivable kind. They are cured in brine or vinegar, or a mixture of the two. The liquor of some pickles is in even greater demand than the pickles themselves. In Adana on the Mediterranean coast for instance, the liquor of pickled turnips is sold in buffets; on hot days in Izmir people buy a pickled cucumber and a refreshing glass of the liquor in the bazaar.

In this recipe I have given a wide choice of vegetables and fruit; use whatever is available, or pickle them separately if you prefer. I like to put some of each fruit and vegetable in each layer so that there is a wide choice.

FOR THE PICKLING LIQUID
1L/1¾ pints white vinegar
25g/1oz salt
VEGETABLES
1kg/2lb cabbage
1kg/2lb gherkins
1kg/2lb courgettes
1kg/2lb pickling onions
1kg/2lb carrots
1kg/2lb long green peppers
2kg/4lb half-ripe tomatoes
100g/3½oz vine leaves
100g/3½oz celeriac
250g/8oz garlic
25g/1oz chickpeas
FRUIT
1kg/2lb quinces
500g/1lb cornelian cherries
500g/1lb medlars (if available)

Mix the vinegar and salt and leave to stand. Clean, wash and drain all the vegetables. Cut the cabbage leaves into small pieces. Top and tail the gherkins and courgettes and prick with a toothpick in several places. Cut the carrots into sticks. Prick the peppers with a toothpick in several places. Cut the celery into sticks, reserving the leaves.

Wash the quinces, core and cut them into quarters. Wash the cornelian cherries and medlars and drain. Put a few vine leaves, a few pieces of celeriac and some chickpeas in the bottom of a large glass or earthenware jar. On top of them put a layer of cabbage leaves. Then add a variety of the vegetables and fruits, filling gaps with garlic cloves, cornelian cherries and medlars. Cover with vine leaves and repeat the layers of leaves, vegetables and fruit until all the ingredients have been used and the jar is full. Cover with vine and celery leaves. Strain the salty vinegar over the contents making sure everything is covered. Put a stone on top to prevent the vegetables rising above the level of the vinegar. Cover the jar and leave at room temperature for 2–3 weeks.

◊ YOĞURT ◊
YOGHURT

Yoghurt has been an essential element of Turkish food since the time when the Turks still lived in Central Asia. Two kinds of yoghurt are used, the semi-liquid known as sıvı tas yoğurt, and a firmer kind called süzme yoğurt. The latter is eaten on its own, or with jam (especially morello cherry jam) in place of a dessert. It is used in all types of cooking, and to make ayran (p.168).

When making yoghurt, if you add 1tbsp of powdered milk to the boiling fresh milk you will get a thicker, firmer yoghurt.

1L/1¾ pints milk
2tbsp thick-set yoghurt

Heat the milk in a heavy pan and when it comes to the boil, lower the heat and sim-mer for 10 minutes. Pour into a bowl and leave on one side until it cools to a temperature bearable to the finger (35–40°C).

Blend the yoghurt with a little of the warm milk, then pour the mixture into the milk and stir well. Cover with a lid and wrap with a towel or blanket. Leave in a warm place for 5–6 hours to ferment and set. Refrigerate when it is ready.

To make süzme yoğurt put 1L/1¾ pints yoghurt into a muslin cloth, gather the four corners to the top and tie in a knot.

Hang up over the sink, or with a bowl underneath, or put it in a colander over a bowl, to drain for 3 hours. You should obtain about 500ml/¾ pint of süzme yoğurt.

◊ PEYNIR ◊
CHEESE

White cheese, beyaz peynir, is the most widely used cheese everywhere in Turkey. It may be fresh and unsalted, or preserved in brine. It is easy to make at home.

2L/3½ pints milk
1tsp cheese rennet

Heat the milk until it reaches a temperature at which it is still bearable to the touch (35°C). Stir in the rennet, cover with a lid and leave to stand in a warm place. It will normally ferment and set within 3½–4 hours. When the milk has coagulated, put it into a muslin or cotton bag, put the bag in a colander with a weight on top and leave to drain for 4–5 hours.

To determine if the cheese has set properly, take a little of the curd between two fingers and squeeze. If the fingers are not smeared with milk it is ready; if there are traces of milk leave to drain longer. To serve, slice the cheese and sprinkle with salt if you wish.

◊ SARIMSAKLI YOĞURT ◊
YOGHURT AND GARLIC SAUCE

500g/1lb thick-set yoghurt
3 cloves garlic (or according to taste)
salt to taste

Put the yoghurt in a bowl. Peel the garlic, and pound it with salt in a mortar until you have a smooth paste. Stir it into the yoghurt and use as required.

◊ TARATOR ◊
TARATOR SAUCE

Tarator is used most extensively in the Aegean region. It may be eaten on its own as a dip and is particularly good with boiled vegetables and plainly cooked fish.

TO SERVE 4–6
50g/2oz shelled walnuts
50g/2oz breadcrumbs
2 cloves of garlic
50ml/2fl oz stock
1tbsp olive oil
50ml/2fl oz vinegar or lemon juice
salt to taste

FOR THE GARNISH
1tbsp olive oil
½tsp red pepper

Pound or mince the walnuts, breadcrumbs and garlic to a paste or blend in a food processor. Add sufficient stock until you achieve the consistency of thick yoghurt. Add the olive oil and vinegar or lemon juice, sprinkle with salt and mix.

Pour the tarator into a dish, pour over the olive oil and sprinkle with red pepper.

◊ DOMATES SALÇASI ◊
TOMATO SAUCE

TO SERVE 6
250g/8oz ripe tomatoes, peeled, deseeded and finely chopped
25ml/1fl oz each olive oil and vinegar
4 cloves of garlic
½tsp each salt and caster sugar

Cook the tomatoes in the oil for about 10 minutes, stirring occasionally, until they absorb their juices. Pound the garlic with the salt and add, followed by the vinegar and sugar. Cover and cook on low heat for 5 minutes, then use as required.

◊ GLOSSARY ◊

Bulgur, or cracked wheat, is available finely or coarsely ground from Middle Eastern shops.

Cornelian cherries, an olive-shaped fruit with a long stone; popular for making jam.

Döğme is a type of wheat flour made from grains that have been soaked in water, then pounded and dried.

Firik is toasted young unripe wheat.

Haspir *(Carthamus tinctorius),* or safflower looks like saffron threads but has a deeper burnt orange colour. It is sprinkled on many Anatolian dishes as a garnish. It will impart colour to a dish as saffron does, but lacks the flavour and aroma of saffron.

Kaşar cheese – hard white cheese made from sheep's milk; substitute an English sheep's milk cheese if you can get one, or a mild cheddar or gouda.

Kaymak is a thick, rich cream used in desserts and baking. Clotted cream is the best substitute.

Lemon salt, or citric acid, is available as crystals. Lemon juice may be substituted.

Mahleb – black cherry kernels ground and used to flavour breads and pastries. Available from Middle Eastern shops.

Mastic – the chewy resin of the acacia tree. It is pulverized (with salt) before being used to flavour meat dishes and desserts.

Nigella *(Nigella sativa),* often erroneously called black onion seed, is a black, peppery seed that is sprinkled on bread and pastries or used in fillings.

Pastırma – cured, air-dried veal, coated with a paste of garlic, cumin and fenugreek that is eaten in thin slices as an appetizer.

Pekmez – thick syrup made from grape juice. A sugar syrup could be used instead but it will lack the flavour of pekmez.

Peppers – the most common capsicums in Turkey are the thin-skinned, narrow, pointed variety, but they should not be confused with green chillies.

Pomegranate syrup – a thick syrup made from the juice of sour pomegranates. Available from Middle Eastern shops.

Red pepper – an essential item in Turkish cooking. It is available powdered or coarsely ground and the taste is not as hot as cayenne nor as mild as paprika. A combination of the two may be used as a substitute. Red pepper appears on the table as a condiment instead of black or white pepper.

Rose water – the diluted essence of rose petals used to flavour desserts, pastries and syrups.

Sübye is a mixture of rice and water used as a basis for milk desserts. The rice is soaked for 8 hours with double the quantity of water (75g to 150ml water); the mixture is then blended and sieved. A blend of ground rice, starch and milk can be used instead, but the dessert may set less well.

Sumac *(Rhus corioria)* – the sour berries of a shrub that grows wild throughout Anatolia. They may be steeped in water and the juice expressed, or ground and used to give a sour note to meat and vegetable dishes. Sumac can be bought in Middle Eastern shops, or use lemon juice as a substitute.

Tahina paste is an oily paste made from crushed sesame seeds.

Verjuice, the juice of unripe grapes, is used in many Anatolian dishes; lemon juice may be substituted.

Wheatstarch (also sold as cream of wheat) is widely used as a thickening agent; cornflour or potato flour may be substituted.

AUTHOR'S ACKNOWLEDGEMENTS

I am indebted to my esteemed friend, Claudia Roden, for her keen interest in Turkish cuisine and her wholehearted assistance in my work, which have greatly contributed to the publication of this book.

To my talented editor, Jill Norman, working with whom was such a pleasure, I express my gratitude both for the interest she has taken in Turkish cuisine and in me personally, and for the help and support she has given me throughout all stages of my work. I regard this book not solely my own work but as the product of our joint endeavours, indeed as our book.

I extend my thanks to Mahmut Samy for undertaking the translation of this work.

I am deeply indebted to my esteemed friend, Gülsen Kahraman, for her generous help in jointly revising the English text.

I wish to thank the Turkish Ministry of Culture and Tourism for providing material support for the photographic work involved, and Timuçin Dulgar of the Ministry's staff for his tireless and patient work in taking the necessary photographs.

I extend my wholehearted thanks to the Chairman of the Board of Management of the Pera Palace Hotel in Istanbul, Hasan Süzer; to the owner of the Konyali Restaurant in Istanbul, Nurettin Doğanbey; to the Chef of the Pandeli Restaurant in Istanbul, Ismail Demir; for their invaluable help. I am also indebted to the Beyti and Urcan restaurants in Istanbul; to the Etap Hotel Restaurant and the Palet Restaurant, both in Izmir; to Ihsan Atasagun and Niyazi Ildirar, both of Konya, and the Konya Tourism Association; to many other individuals and foundations for their assistance in similar work, and to any number of street hawkers too numerous to name here.

I extend my special thanks to my esteemed cookery teacher colleagues in Izmir, Cemile Sezen, Nevin Yilmaz and Serpil Altay, from whose knowledge and expertise I benefited during our professional work together; to my esteemed cookery teacher in England, Mrs Janet Meyrick of Brighton, who helped me in identifying foodstuffs and ingredients.

I wish to thank Nilgün Çelebi, Aziz Kaplan and Yakup Çelik and many others, all natives of Konya, who helped me with different points of detail in the book.

For having helped me in tasting dishes described in this book when I prepared them with ingredients I had brought over from England, I wish to express my thanks above all to my mother, Halıcı Hanım, that supreme cook and gourmet and my first and foremost teacher in my training as a chef, and to my brothers Feyzi, Metin and Hasan, and my sister Nermin.

I also extend my thanks to the publishers Dorling Kindersley Ltd., for publishing my book and those members of its staff concerned.

INDEX

◊ BIBLIOGRAPHY ◊

BOOKS

AHSAN, M M: *Social Life Under the Abbasids*, London 1979.

ALI RIZA BEY: *Old Times In Istanbul* (ed Niyazi Ahmet Banoğlu) Tercuman.

ARAT, RAŞIT RAHMETI: *Book of Knowledge III* (ed Kemal Eraslan & Osman Sertkaya) 1979.

DAVID, ELIZABETH: *A Book of Mediterranean Food*, London, Penguin Books 1978.

DE BUSBECG, OGIER GHISELIN: *Turkey As I Saw It* (ed Aysel Kurutluoglu) Tercuman.

D'OHSSON, M DE M: *Customs and Habits In 18th-Century Turkey* (trs by Zerhan Yüksel) Tercuman.

ERTÜRK, NECIP: *The Art Of Turkish Cooking*, Istanbul, Kral Press 1976.

ERTÜRK, NECIP: *The Art Of Turkish Dessert Making*, Istanbul, Kral Press 1978.

EVLIYA, CELEBI: *Selections From A Travelogue* (ed Atsiz) Istanbul, Milli Eğitim Press 1972.

EYUBOĞLU, ISMET ZEKI: *Anatolian Civilization*, DER Publications.

FULTON, MARGARET: *Encyclopaedia Of Food And Cookery*, Octopus Books 1985.

GELIBOLULU, MUSTAFA ALI: *Lunch And Dinner Party Arrangements* (ed Orhan Şaik Gökyay) Istanbul, Tercuman.

GÖLPINARLI, ABDULBAKI: *Mevlevi Ceremonies and Rites*, Istanbul, Yeni Press 1963.

GÜREL, RAŞIT: *Home Cooking* Vols I, II, III & IV (2nd edition) Ankara, Fon Press 1972.

HACIP, YUSUF HAS: *Book Of Knowledge* (ed A Dilaçar) Ankara, Turkish Language Institute Publications 1972.

HAJIB, YUSUF KHAŞŞ: *Wisdom Of Royal Glory: A Turco-Islamic Mirror For Princes* (trs Robert Dankoff) Chicago and London, The University of Chicago Press 1983.

HALICI, FEYZI: *Istanbul Boulevard*, Istanbul, Şehir Press 1956.

HALICI, FEYZI (ED): *Traditional Turkish Dishes and Nutrition*, Konya, Doğuş Press 1982.

HALICI, NEVIN: *Mediterranean Region Dishes*, Konya, Ari Press 1983.

HALICI, NEVIN: *Aegean Region Dishes*, Ankara, Güven Press 1981.

HALICI, NEVIN: *Traditional Konya Dishes*, Ankara, Güven Press 1979.

HALICI, NEVIN: *Turkish Cookery*, Ankara, Güven Press 1985.

KARAMAN, HAYREDDIN: *The Canonically Prohibited and Permissible In Our Daily Life*, Istanbul, Elif Offset Printing Press 1981.

KARABULUT, OSMAN: *The Virtues Of Holy Months, Days And Nights*, Konya, Sebat Press.

KOŞAY, Z HAMIT & ÜLKÜCAN, AKILE: *Anatolian Dishes & Turkish Cuisine*, Ankara, Milli Eğitim Press 1961.

KOŞAY, Z HAMIT & ÜLKÜCAN, AKILE: *The Holy Koran And Its Turkish Meaning*, Ankara, Directorate of Religious Affairs 1961.

KUT, GÜNAY: *How To Prepare Desserts*, Ankara, Feryal Press 1985.

KUT, TURGUT: *Bibliography Of Cookery Books*, Ankara, Feryal Press 1985

MAHMUD, KAŞGARLI: *Classical Turkish Dictionary* (trs Besim Atalay) Ankara, Turkish Historical Society Press 1985.

MEVLANA, CELALEDDIN: *Divani Kebir* (ed Abdülbaki Gölpinarli), Istanbul, Yüskelen Press 1957.

MEVLANA, CELALEDDIN: *Rubailer* (ed Abdülbaki Gölpinarli) Ankara, Ajans Türk Press 1982.

MEVLANA, CELALEDDIN: *Mesnevi Ve Şerhi* (annotated by Abdülbaki Gölpinarli) Istanbul, Milli Eğitim Press 1985 (2nd edition).

MÜTERCIM, ASIM EFENDI: *El-Okyanus El-basit Ti Tercümeti'l Kaamus* Vol.II, Istanbul, 1250/1834.

ÖGEL, BAHAEDDIN: *Introduction To The History Of Turkish Culture*, Book 4, Istanbul, Milli Eğitim Press 1978.

ORHAN, ŞAIK GÖKYAY (ED): *Tales Of Dede Korkut*, Istanbul, Milli Eğitim Press 1973.

ÖRNEK, SEDAT VEYIS: *The Place Of Children In Our Traditional Culture*, Ankara, Saim Toraman Press 1979.

SEFERCIOĞLU, NECAT: *Turkish Dishes (A Manual of 18th-Century Cookery)* Ankara, Feryal Press 1985.

TAVERNIER, J B: *Life At The Topkapı Palace*, Istanbul, Can Press 1984.

UNGER, FRIEDRICH: *The Sweet Makers Of The East* (ed Feyzi Halıcı) Konya, Culture & Tourism Association.

ÜNVER, SÜHEYL: *Dishes Of The Fatih (Conqueror) Period*, Istanbul, Kemal Press 1952.

YEĞEN, EKREM MUHIDDIN: *Instruction In Turkish And Western Meal Arrangements And Table Manners*, Istanbul, Yelken Press 1977.

YEĞEN, EKREM MUHIDDIN: *Instruction in Turkish And Western Sweets And Pastry, Cold Dishes, Mezes and Salads*, Istanbul, Inkilap ve Aka Press 1977.

ARTICLES

ERTÜRK, NECIP: Turkish Cuisine, *Milliyet* 2.12.1972.

FELEK, BURHAN: Turkish Cuisine 75-100 Years Ago (Part 1), *Milliyet* 21.8.1977.

FELEK, BURHAN: Ramadhan Meals – *Milliyet* 19.9.1976.

GENÇ, REŞAT: Turkish Cookery In The 19th Century, Papers of the Turkish Culinary Art Symposium, Ankara University Press 1982.

GÜLERSOY, TUNCER: On Food Terms Used By Tatar Turks, Papers of the Turkish Culinary Art Symposium, Ankara University Press 1982.

HALICI, FEYZI: Turkish Cookery From The Neolithic Age To Contemporary Times And Its Place In Our Sacred Customs, Papers of the Turkish Culinary Art Symposium, Ankara University Press 1982.

HALICI, NEVIN: Anatolian Cookery, Papers of the Turkish Culinary Art Symposium, Ankara University Press 1982. Konya Dishes & Offerings for Celebrations, *Fresh Look at Turkish Popular Culture and Folklore Part I* (ed Feyzi Halıcı) Ankara Güven Press 1985.

KUT GÜNAY: Cookery Book Of 13th-Century Cooking Vol. III, Istanbul 1984.

KUT, GÜNAY: Researches Into Folklore and Ethnography, Istanbul 1985.

ONGUN, ZARIF: Table Manners At The Ottoman Palace, Papers of the Turkish Culinary Art Symposium, Ankara University Press 1982.

ÜNVER, SÜHEYL: Meals During The Seljuk, Principalities And Ottoman Periods, Papers of the Turkish Culinary Art Symposium, Ankara University Press 1982.